The Disinherited

Also by Margaret Simey from Liverpool University Press

Charity Rediscovered: A Study of Charitable Effort in Nine-teenth-century Liverpool, 1992, reprint of 1951 with a new Prologue by the author.

MARGARET SIMEY

The Disinherited Society

A PERSONAL VIEW OF SOCIAL RESPONSIBILITY IN LIVERPOOL
DURING THE TWENTIETH CENTURY

LIVERPOOL UNIVERSITY PRESS

First published 1996 by
LIVERPOOL UNIVERSITY PRESS
Senate House
Abercromby Square
Liverpool
L69 3BX

British Library Cataloguing-in-Publication Data
A British Library CIP record is available

ISBN 0-85323-800-6

Typeset by Wilmaset Ltd, Birkenhead, Wirral
Printed and bound in the European Union by
Page Bros (Norwich) Ltd.

PREFACE

It is customary to include in a book of this kind a list of all those to whom the writer is indebted for stimulus or guidance. If I fail to do so, it is not from any lack of gratitude to the many who have, perhaps unwittingly, contributed to my blundering search after understanding. Rather it is because I wish to emphasise the magnitude of my debt to that regiment of the nameless to whom I owe such wisdom as I have acquired. It is to the unsung men and women of the inner city who strive so unceasingly for the betterment of others and whom it has been my good fortune to encounter that I take this opportunity to pay my most sincere tribute.

Finally, I must record my profound gratitude to my husband. It was by the happiest of chances that, in the context of this book which is all about the interlock between the women's movement and the search for urban democracy, I should have been enabled to explore that very issue with him in terms of our own lives. The moral and philosophical content of his approach to the process of social change added immensely to my comprehension of my own quest for personal fulfilment in a world of ambiguities and injustices that I find hard to understand.

CONTENTS

Introduction

CAUSE FOR CONCERN 1

In which I set out my intention as being to present the search for democracy in the urban society of the twentieth century in terms of my own experience in Liverpool. I do so in the hope of contributing to the regeneration of commitment to the principle of universal social responsibility as an attribute of citizenship.

Part One

THE CREED AND THE CRAFT
OF SOCIAL RESPONSIBILITY

Chapter 1   THE ATHENS OF THE NORTH 15

In which I discover that Liverpool's claim to be the Athens of the North was countered by the existence of chronic poverty in the midst of exceptional wealth. This was exacerbated by its dependence on the River, hence what Eleanor Rathbone described as the extremely peculiar constitution of its population and the consequent intensity of its social problems.

Chapter 2   THE CREED OF SOCIAL RESPONSIBILITY 25

In which I describe how the turn of the century saw the unique coming together in Liverpool of the moral commitment of the merchant community, the idealism of the young University and the passion of the women's demand for equal citizenship. Their Urban Ideal embodied the principle of universal social responsibility.

the realisation that nevertheless, I was getting nowhere. Sound administration is not enough; it must be fuelled by the political will to act. I determine to become a City Councillor.

In which first-hand experience of life in the Granby ward in Toxteth focuses my attention on the practicalities of community development. My commitment to the principle of universal social responsibility is constantly refreshed by my involvement in local affairs as an elected member.

In which the application of business management to local government fails to resolve the deepening crisis in the inner cities and facilitates the take-over of the administration of community affairs by the bureaucracy. This resulted in the extrusion of the elected representative and the deprivation of the right of the individual to social responsibility. Granby becomes a disinherited society.

In which I reflect on my experience as Chairman of Merseyside Policy Authority following on the 1981 riots. Responsibility for what was done in our name by the police emphasised the importance of accountability. I revert to voluntary action and discover that democracy is to be rediscovered at the grass roots.

Part Two

In which I argue that the experience of the past century confirms the validity of the principle of the right to social responsibility as a fundamental attribute of universal citizenship. The time has come for a New Emancipation Movement committed to the creation of a Welfare Society of which the Welfare State will be the instrument whereby those privileges will become the daily experience of every citizen.

Introduction

CAUSE FOR CONCERN

In which I set out my intention as being to present the search for democracy in the urban society of the twentieth century in terms of my own experience in Liverpool. I do so in the hope of contributing to the regeneration of commitment to the principle of universal social responsibility as an attribute of citizenship.

I had the singular good fortune when young to come under the influence of that band of trojan women who, led by Eleanor Rathbone, operated under the banner of the Liverpool Women Citizens' Association. Their purpose was to win for women the right to vote in order that they might enjoy the full responsibilities of citizenship and to train them to carry out the obligations this would impose upon them. It was to that end that they demanded the right to education, to opportunity, to independence. Whatever their particular needs, the common inspiration which bound them all together was the passion of their conviction that each and every one of them had a right and a duty to take their place as contributing members of the community to which they belonged. Active Citizens indeed!

It is impossible to convey to the 1990s the long-lasting impact of that declaration on me and my generation in the period after the First World War. We were that unfortunate band who faced life dubbed 'Superfluous Women'. The label was deadly accurate. We were literally superfluous; superfluous to the needs of a marriage market sharply diminished by the consequences of war, superfluous on the economic market where the long shadow of the Great Slump already cast a gloom over all our lives. Unwanted even on the home front since to keep unmarried daughters in idleness was a luxury many middle-class families could no longer afford. And politically of no account. (I still remember, sixty years on, the precise moment when, for the first time ever, I cast my vote in a polling booth.) Miraculously, these Women Citizens turned our resentment against the injustice of our condemnation to futility and frustration into a moral conviction which totally redeemed our situation. Our salvation lay in their undeviating loyalty to the principle of the universal right of every member of the community to play their part as responsible citizens. This above all else justified our existence.

Nor were women alone in this commitment for what marked out the early years of the century in Liverpool was the emergence of a unique vision of what it might mean to be a citizen in an urban democracy. It was not only women who must be set free to make their contribution to the society in which they lived; the poor must be emancipated from their poverty in order that they too might exercise their right to the full responsibilities of citizenship. This remarkable break with the traditional patronage of the charitable owed its inspiration to the coming together of the idealism of the academics at the young University with the practical morality of the city's merchant philanthropists. Infused as both were by the passion and urgency of the women's demand for liberation, the result was the fresh approach to the social problems of the day on which the dream of Liverpool as the New Athens of the North was founded. Every single person, simply by virtue of their common humanity and regardless of merit, sex, religion or any other qualification, was entitled to lay claim to the obligations as well as the benefits of citizenship. It was the duty of society to ensure that this high-minded principle was viable in practise.

The nub of this astonishing extension of the idea of citizenship—astonishing even now but much more so in the context of a city notorious for its poverty—lay in the novel concept of citizenship as a two-way relationship between the individual and society. The universal right to enjoy the benefits of membership of the community must be matched by the opportunity to share in the responsibility for the management of the affairs of that community. To give as well as to receive must be made the daily experience of every citizen, for it was only in that way that the individual could draw from the common pool as well as contribute to it without harm being done to either. This was my heritage, this the distant horizon towards which all the years of my life have been directed.

How different the scene as the century draws to a close. Those of us who were in at the birth of the Welfare State that was the fruit of that early endeavour can only eye with bewildered disbelief the pass to which we have come: the rank individualism, the materialism, the narrowing focus of human endeavour on me and mine and, chillingly, the prospect that we will eventually be reduced to caring for 'me' alone. Of the dream of building a new urban society little remains. The century that started out with such high hopes of transforming Liverpool into the Athens of the North has ended with that which is most to be feared in a democracy, the voluntary submission by a politically ignorant people to relegation to an underclass. Certainly the battle has been won in so far as the right of women to work in what is still regarded as a man's world has been generally recognised, though escape from the bondage of the tradition of domesticity remains to be achieved. Certainly the worst stresses and strains of the struggle for individual survival have been relieved.

But what of the original purpose for which women fought with such determination, the glorious vision of the universal right to social responsibility? How barren the inheritance into which we have entered. All passion seems to have been spent. The very idea of active citizenship has become so remote from reality that we have to be exhorted to do our civic duty by clergy and politicians alike. (So much so that when in 1986 the abolition of the Metropolitan County Councils took from those who lived in them their right to vote in the County elections, few seemed to care. What to us had been a privilege beyond price appeared to be of no more worth than the old paper pound is today.)

Indeed, the entire process of government, of the management of our common affairs that we call politics, is seen as largely irrelevant to the lives of ordinary people except as an obstacle to be circumvented whenever possible. Government is not by consent but by remote control. 'They' who govern have somehow been permitted to take from 'Us', the governed, our birthright of responsibility. We have been conditioned to acquiesence, reduced to subservience, all by due process of what passes for democracy. Ours not to reason why, ours but to pay up and shut up, as I was once bluntly advised by the police. All that we are required to do is concentrate on getting the best we can for those popularly called our loved ones and, ultimately, for ourselves alone. The vision of a welfare society has given way to the reality of a state system of benefits, demanded as of right and grudgingly accorded. At the end of the road for all of us lies the prospect of an old age lived out in the loneliness of an uncaring community. The poverty of politics that this should be so!

However can this have come about? Was it the vision of an urban democracy that failed us or have we failed the vision? Can it be that democracy—the democracy the women's movement pursued with such zeal—is a luxury we can no longer afford and must learn to do without? Or, in moments of darkest despair which some would call realism, maybe we have to accept that the whole democratic thing is a played-out fantasy and that we are in fact the helpless and hopeless victims of the ebb and flow of economic tides whose manipulation is controlled by those faceless monsters, the international corporations? In which case, there is nothing for it but a clean sweep of capitalism and all its wicked ways, if we are to remedy the injustices we see all about us. 'Up the revolution' will be the cry.

It is a well-worn cliché to claim that only by seeing the present in the light of the past can there be any hope of making sense of the future. Yet what possible relevance can this tale of days gone by, however fascinating, have to the unprecedentedly unpredictable prospect which we now contemplate? However noble in principle the assertion of the universal right of the individual to share in the common responsibility, is it really viable in the context of this particular day and age? What guidance can it possibly hold out for the future?

The question takes on an added urgency by reason of the challenge of the contract culture to the very tradition of voluntary action itself, uttered with such dogmatic fervour by the Conservative government. The voluntary movement must forget its charitable origins, we are assured: the voluntary services have been selected for commercialisation and their supporters must equip themselves to fulfil that high destiny if they are to maintain their claim to public support. Charity, they tell us, is a medieval concept that has no contribution to make to the economy of the market place. 'There is no such thing as society', an ex-Prime Minister once declared.

The lesson of the past would, indeed, seem to be that the dream of a responsible society is a science fiction fantasy. It is all too easy to believe that we have no option but to resign ourselves to life in the shrinking territory that is all our managers have left us. Given the embattled front presented by the huge ramifications of the bureaucracy (of which I had searing experience in my encounter with the police when I was Chairman of the Merseyside Police Authority), together with the grip of selfish materialism on public morality, the question for us today is no longer that of whether the principle of universal social responsibility is sound or not but whether in the world as it is, it is a practical proposition. Not only have we lost our faith in the vision but even the vision itself.

As we face the future, bewildered and at a loss, one thing is for sure. There can be no going back to 'the good old days' of nostalgic memory. What we are living through is not the end of a recession but the end of an era. There is no realistic hope of unpicking the complex interlock of the system of government with which we are now cumbered, no question of resuscitating the old code of political morality from which government derived its marching orders. We are refugees from the twentieth century who embark on an unknown future with no more mental luggage than a suitcaseful of memories. We have outgrown our past.

Nor can we stand still in this time of political turbulence. To do nothing would be to commit ourselves to going on down the road that Beveridge described as 'the primrose path to mutual destruction' (William Beveridge,

Power and Influence, London, Hodder & Stoughton, 1952). The discord bred by enforced competition for grant aid for the inner cities is a sad demonstration of the accuracy of his forecast. Given the climate of the times, there is nothing for it but to face up to whatever the future holds for us, a singularly intimidating prospect for the simple reason that we have lost our sense of direction.

Nevertheless, just as I am confident that there can be no going back, so too, I am equally confident that if we are to move forward with a clear sense of direction, we can only do so on the basis of a respect for the lessons of the past, something that is singularly lacking from the approach to social policy by the decision-makers of today. What then, has the story I have told to contribute to the situation in which we currently find ourselves?

Now, as at the beginning of the century, the issue is one of how we who live in an urban society are to order our common affairs. It is in that context that we face the recurrent dilemma of every human community—the apparently irreconcilable contradiction between the right to personal freedom and the obligations of membership of a community. What I have to offer is a case history of that search for urban democracy in terms of the lives of the people whose doings I recount, and of my own. It is my hope that by recalling the vision which is our inheritance from them, I may make a modest contribution to the regeneration of the enthusiasm for social change that inspired them. I am convinced that only by learning from the past can we face the future with the courage and conviction it will surely require.

This laudable intention is, however, likely to be frustrated by the simple fact that, outside academic circles, the world at large is simply not interested in the lessons of the past. Old wives' tales, such as those that I have to tell, are seen as suitable material for nostalgic programmes on television but they are not thought to have any practical relevance to the problems of today. It is a truism to which the inner cities bear sad witness that 'we never learn'. I am constantly amazed by the abysmal ignorance, especially amongst those who are responsible for decision making, as to how we got from where we started out to where we now are, and the consequent inability to foresee what will happen next. There is a widespread failure to grasp the implications for the future of this devaluation of past experience. Time like an ever-rolling stream bears all our sons—and daughters—away and with them go all the acquired wisdom of their experience, to our great loss. The consequences are dire. As a society, we are now setting out on our journey into the new world of the next century with no other maps or signposts than a miscellaneous collection of assumptions, prejudices and good intentions. For lack of a sense of continuity, we find ourselves adrift on a sea of uncertainty. Every situation, every crisis has to be tackled from scratch. All the old mistakes have to be made all over again before we even get round to breaking new ground. 'We've been here before' is the common cry but it never seems to provoke thought as to what lessons could be learned that would rescue us from the vicious circle in which we seem to be trapped.

I believe it to be no exaggeration to claim that this indifference to the potential of our inheritance as a guide to the future is one of the major contributions to the political malaise from which we currently suffer. Political decisions are taken without reference to the past circumstances from which the current situation has developed. Policies are formulated at random regardless of the context, past or present, to which they must apply. The success of a democratic system depends on the level of the education of the 'meanest he' amongst us: it is our failure to ensure that as a society we are educated to have a grasp of all that goes to make up our social heritage that is at the root of the current alienation of government from governed. The past should serve as the launching pad into the future. Only by taking a backward look at the past will we be enabled to retrieve the sense of purpose for lack of which we now falter.

It is as a contribution to breaking through that dangerous habit of thought that I present this book. It is not an academic study, though I hope it will be of interest to students of social history. I give few references to books by other people though I fear that my magpie mind stores away for future use ideas for which I owe them thanks. Instead, I have deliberately restricted myself to the evidence of the innumerable people I have encountered along the way to whose first-hand experience I owe such wisdom as I have acquired. My aim is to rouse interest in the lessons to be learned from the past and to stimulate an awareness of their relevance to the future. I have chosen to do this in terms of charitable effort in Liverpool in the twentieth century as I myself knew it, because I believe that to be a method specifically suited to my purpose.

I draw on my personal experience of the events I describe not out of conceit but rather the opposite. My theme is the struggle to achieve a satisfactory relationship between each and every one of us and the society of which we are contributory members. How better to illustrate the disparity between the puny David that is the individual citizen and the Goliath of the state than to describe it in terms of a single human experience? I am my own visual aid. As an inch is to a mile, so a life is to a century. It is my hope that by using my own life as a frame of reference, I will be able to convey to others my own strong sense of the continuity of human endeavour and of the relevance of past history to future planning.

My choice of title merits a word of explanation. Eleanor Rathbone called her book on family allowances *The Disinherited Family* (London, Edward Arnold, 1924), but the significance of the title has been ignored. She herself only once volunteered any comment:

> The term Family Endowment—one of unknown parentage, and not, it must be confessed, particularly felicitous—does not stand for any concrete scheme. It stands for a principle, viz. that the economic structure of Society should include some kind of direct provision for the financial cost of rearing children ... The community must provide somehow for the rearing of fresh generations. (E. Rathbone, *The Ethics and Economics of Family Endowment*, Social Service Lecture Trust, Epworth Press, 1927)

To Eleanor, the injustice of the dependent status of women as mothers was an offence against their human dignity that amounted to a denial of the individual's rightful inheritance. The duty to rectify this must rest on the community as a whole. The scheme for family allowances was, in fact, simply a practical expression of her lifelong commitment to the fundamental principle that personal fulfilment could only be achieved in the context of a supportive society, the creation of which must be a collective responsibility.

I echo her choice partly as a tribute to the insight that inspired her to that grasp of a basic social principle far in advance of her times, but partly also because the change from 'family' to 'society' so neatly encapsulates the essence of the account I have given of subsequent events. By and large, the century that is now closing has seen the gradual acceptance of the principle that a society has obligations to its members. It is our failure to comprehend the implications of putting that principle into practice that justifies the description of our as a disinherited society. As a community we are denied our right to social responsibility. The future lies in the exploration of ways and means of rectifying this so that we may enter into our rightful heritage.

Why 1909? Why Liverpool? Why me? Quite apart from the sentiment that always attaches to the turn of a century, the first decade of the twentieth century was dominated by an especially strong sense of threshold, of the ending of one era and the inevitability of the far-reaching changes which the future would bring. Nowhere was this more evident than in regard to the social condition of the people. The continuing existence of poverty on a massive scale in the midst of evident affluence presented a singularly baffling problem and the turn of the century was marked by a growing awareness of the fact that a totally new approach to its solution would have to be devised. This was, of course, a concern that was universal, hence the setting-up in 1906 of the Royal Commission on the Poor Law.

The situation, was, however, peculiarly acute in Liverpool because there the stark contrast between the two worlds of rich and poor was not softened by any of the patina of age and tradition that graced the social structure of older towns like Bristol. On the one hand, the gentleman, however modest his income: on the other, the labourer, sometimes perversely loyal to his tradition of poverty and arrogant in his ignorance. Nowhere else than Liverpool did the apparently chronic existence of poverty present a greater challenge to the enjoyment of plentitude.

Look about the city to this day and you see everywhere monuments to the spirit of civic pride that reached its peak at the turn of the century. The foundation stone of the gigantic Anglican Cathedral was laid by Edward VII in 1902, that of the Catholic soon after. The modest college on Brownlow Hill achieved its charter as a University in that same year. The Mersey Docks and Harbour Board built its grandiose head offices at the Pierhead in 1912, all mosaics and custom-built furniture for which they were to be hard pressed to pay. Andrew Carnegie personally visited the city to unveil plaques of beaten copper studded with enamels in the art nouveau public libraries which decorated the inner areas. The Holts sailed the Nile in their private yacht. The Rathbone family rented a castle on Windermere for their summer holidays. Yet still the poor were ever with them, providing a chronically insecure foundation for the grandeur that was Liverpool, a reproach to the social conscience, a burden on the civic purse, a threat to the health and well-being of the whole community.

It was a problem to which the Royal Commission struggled for years to find an answer, in vain. Nevertheless, the eventual publication of its Report in 1909 (Royal Commission on the Poor Law, cd 4499, London, HMSO, 1909), although in itself no great work, served to release in Liverpool a flood tide of new ideas, new visions and fresh energies which went far beyond finding ways and means of expressing the traditional charitable relationship. Because of the desperate necessity of the challenge of poverty as presented in the city, the response it provoked there was a peculiarly brilliant one. It was generally beginning to be accepted—though with extreme reluctance by many—that an increasing share of the responsibility for the provision for those in need would have to be yielded up to the state. Remarkably, there were those in

Liverpool who realised that the implication of this must be that the right to responsibility for what was done by the state in the name of the people must be a universal attribute of citizenship.

It is with that vision of what citizenship in a great industrial city should and could be, and the lasting commitment of Liverpool men and women to its implementation as I myself witnessed it that my story is concerned.

Why me? Looking back over the way I have come, I am struck by the fact that my life has been a close reflection of that of the society in which I have lived. I am essentially a product of my times. By chance, my own existence exactly spans the period which saw the birth, the full flowering and the eventual fading of the vision of the Welfare State. Seen from the peak of my old age, it makes a satisfyingly neat package. I do not delude myself that the part I played as an individual was of any special significance, but the fact is that I walked the boards of the stage whereon the saga was enacted. This was my life. I knew the leading players, I heard them speak their parts. It was through my own eyes that I saw the events about which this book is written.

I was born in Glasgow in 1906 (shortly after the appointment of the Royal Commission on the Poor Law), but most of my life has been lived elsewhere, my father being forced, as were so many Scots, to look abroad for opportunity. By happy chance, his appointment as head of a further education college brought us to Liverpool just as I left school. There I promptly found myself enlisted as an 'apprentice' to Eleanor Rathbone, myself one of that first generation of emancipated women who owed our opportunity to the women's movement. At that time, the School of Social Science at the University was one of the pioneers of the scientific study of social problems, and when their endeavours were recognised by the endowment of a Professorial Chair and the setting up of a degree course in Social Science, I was the first student to enrol.

Almost all of my adult life since then has been spent in Liverpool, much of it actually living in the hard core of Toxteth. I knew at first-hand the guilt and shame of the Great Depression of the 1930s. As a middle-class wife and mother, I have always been actively involved in the amazing enthusiasm for voluntary action that is characteristic of the city to this day. Through my husband, who became Professor of Social Science at the University, I came to know many of the men and women who were in the forefront of the development of social science. When eventually I moved into party politics as a Labour Councillor, I was elected by Granby, the very ward in Toxteth that Eleanor Rathbone had represented when she became Liverpool's first woman Councillor. My subsequent experience as a County Councillor and

Chairman of the Merseyside Police Authority added a dimension to my life that left me constantly amazed. 'Can this be really me?', I used to cry out in disbelief.

Now rising ninety, I am often asked what it is that has powered my ability to keep on trying, in spite of disappointment and disillusion so that I am, I understand, talked of as 'Old Indestructible'. Faced with such a scenario of doom and gloom as confronts us today, I can only answer that it is the vindication by experience of my loyalty to the vision of my inheritance that is my salvation. I started out with no more than a warm heart and an angry resentment against injustice. Maturity has firmed that up into a positive commitment to the creation of a society in which not one person suffers the injustice of the denial of the right to share in the common responsibility for the well-being of the community as a whole. It is because we who live in urban conurbations have abandoned the pursuit of the principles and practice of living together as a human society that we find ourselves in our current state of dreadful unease.

It is on that same basis of first-hand contact with real people and real situations that I have come to realise that this is no dream but the most practical of possibilities. The dogged persistence with which all manner of people in all manner of circumstances have refused to be deterred from 'loving their neighbour' has been an example which has enabled me to survive many hard times.

I am confident that the problems of democratic governance that beset us today will only be resolved if they are steadfastly founded on the fundamental principle that government by consent is necessarily government by the people. It is to the ordinary citizen that we must look for our deliverance. This is the insight into the practice of politics that has constantly refreshed my own energies.

It is the blistering heat of that conviction at which I have now arrived that drives me to write this book and gives me the confidence that the theme I so assiduously pursue is relevant to the desperate need of our times for a restatement of age-old principles in terms of today and tomorrow. My hope is that I may be able to pass on to others something of the sense of purpose and inspiration that has endowed my own life with a significance far beyond anything that I as an individual ever hoped to achieve and for lack of which I would surely have been defeated.

Part One

THE CREED AND THE CRAFT OF SOCIAL RESPONSIBILITY

Chapter 1
THE ATHENS OF THE NORTH

In which I discover for myself that Liverpool's proud claim to be
the Athens of the North was countered by the existence of chronic
poverty in the midst of exceptional wealth. This was exacerbated
by its dependence on the River; hence what Eleanor Rathbone
described as 'the extremely peculiar constitution' of its population
and the consequent intensity of its social problems.

I start with myself at the age of seventeen, trundling over the Runcorn railway
bridge towards Liverpool through the rain of a dirty winter's night in the early
nineteen twenties. Street lamps shone in the deserted little township below
the viaduct. There was a gleam of reflected light on the sweep of the sand flats,
left bare by the receding tide. Suddenly, the gates of Hell opened. Furnaces,
pinpoints of fierce flame, chimneys belching visible fumes, the fearful smell
of rotten eggs. All my London veneer, my public school culture, the sophistication of my childhood in Cairo, all of it vanished, and I found myself gulp-
ing with excitement. 'This is real . . . this is *real.*'

Where on earth that excitement had its origins, goodness only knows. I
had dabbled in girls' club work (a romantic Minnehaha sort of organisation
called the Camp Fire Girls, imported from America), but only in Ealing where
poverty and injustice—'reality'—were hard to come by. So why this sudden
upsurge of passion about Liverpool being 'real'? Long years of the suppres-
sion of every emotion at the hands of the dedicated spinsters at St Paul's Girls'
School, in the enclosed life of a pupil at a girls-only public school, no doubt
played their part. Whatever, here now was this glorious feeling of sudden and
unexpected escape, of a way out from a prison I didn't even know I was in.

That could be written off as an exaggeration but for the fact that that first
impression was never to be challenged, although it has taken a long time—all
the rest of the time I have had—to discover what it is that endows life in Liverpool with that quality of reality, which binds so many of us to her. All of us,
that is, who don't turn tail and flee from the place as rapidly as opportunity
allows. There is a University anecdote about a man from Cambridge who was

invited for lunch (as was the University custom when considering the appointment of a new professor), with a view to being offered the Chair of Social Science. He is said to have got out of the train, taken one look at Lime Street, and stepped smartly back in again to return from whence he came. My husband was eventually appointed in his stead.

I don't recollect anything much of my early impressions of Waterloo, our riverside suburb. Peering away back to those days of long ago, I remember only a soft blur of sands and tides, a grey stillness—the Bootle Cow bellowing out its warning through the fog to ships at the river mouth: the salt smell of the sea, even in the city's streets: and the ships, always the ships. It didn't feel like London, not the suburban Ealing I knew, anyhow. Our lives here were dominated by the river. The tide and the weather literally governed our daily routine: according to their state, we went out of the front door and along the sea-front, or out of the back gate to hug the shelter of the high garden walls. My father kept a leather-bound brass telescope at the ready in his study window, with a Chamber of Commerce sheet of *Ships, their Funnels and their Flags* pinned up beside it for ready reference. Not that we needed it. We quickly became more familiar with the house colours of the different shipping companies and the flags of the countries they came from than we were with the numbers and routes of the trams in town.

Our house was one of a rather grandiose terrace facing onto Liverpool Bay at the point where the Mersey joined with the Dee to flood over a vast seascape of sandbanks and channels. From it, we could see all the way to the Welsh hills and the Snowdon range, and right out to the Bar Lightship and the open sea. The sunsets were stupendous, the variety of cloud and colour and sky a perpetual fascination. Our terrace dated from the days of Victorian suburban expansion. It had cornices and curlicues and iron-trellised verandahs—all in a rather 'gossy' stucco, to use a good Scots word meaning imposing in a conspicuous sort of way. Across the road, right on the sands, was the common garden, like a London square, though it was far from common and zealously locked up to keep out the poor who lived in the back streets.

All very imposing and deliberately so because a town that depended on credit for the conduct of its affairs must necessarily create a good impression. The rest of Waterloo dated from an earlier age when it had provided a seaside bolthole for the women and children of the merchant class during the fever-laden summer months. As transport improved, it had been replaced in popularity by classier places across the river on the Wirral and down the coast at Southport, so that, by the time we got there, it was becoming seedy (though our neighbours on one side still kept a butler).

What went for us as a family was true then of the whole great sprawling city. Its life was focused on the River. You couldn't even find your way about till you grasped the fact that the streets radiated out from a now non-existent Pool, long since drained. Even the trams all gathered at the Pier Head, nose to the river like cattle in a drought. You knew it was Friday night because of the flush of cabs running passengers from the stations to the great steamships tied up at the Pierhead, ready to catch the evening tide. The streets had names literally out of the sea shanties we sang at school. The ships paraded up and down the river like traffic on a motorway, Kipling's Empire exemplified. There could be no failure to grasp the point. This was a Port, a Great Port, and ominously nothing but a Port.

At the time it all seemed exhilaratingly romantic. Kipling and Masefield were our gods and heroes, with their tales of dirty tin tubs battling their way through heavy seas on the way to far-flung ports. It wasn't till the early thirties dragged us all into the pit of mass unemployment that the hideous potential of the dependence on the River struck home to our hearts. If the River failed us, we had nothing else. Our bread and butter, our homes and hearths, the whole fabric of our society and our way of life—all these originated in our dependence on the River. It was because of the River that many of us had come here in the first place. If the River didn't need us, then who did?

All that was yet to come. Meanwhile we wallowed in sentimental pride in the Glory That Was Liverpool. We didn't take our visitors to see the countryside, unless you count going to see the Grand National at Aintree as a rural outing. Our pride was in our urbanity. Runtling along the Docks in the old Overhead Railway with its hard slatted seats, spotting unusual cargoes coming in from abroad or lying on the dockside in the rain, waiting to be loaded on an out-going steamer. Going to New Brighton on the ferry: that was an urban outing if ever there was one, not remotely like the summer holiday at the seaside of my childhood. Even the mandatory day at Southport, for which best clothes must be worn, was no escapist jaunt: Southport was an appendage of the rich of Manchester and Liverpool, tangible evidence of our commercial success.

There was, of course, no past to show off. This was no medieval city in the good old English tradition. There was no castle here, except on a street name plate, no remnant of the great forest of Toxteth where King John once hunted, other than a street named Lodge Lane where once a shelter had stood but which acquired notoriety in the 1981 disturbances as the scene of unparalleled looting. In an uncharacteristic gesture of cynicism, my husband insisted on having a symbolic tree inserted in his coat of arms when he became Lord Simey of Toxteth.

But if we had no past, what a glory was the present. The trio of buildings which constituted the distinctive profile of the Pier Head were all evidence of the opulence of our success. The Mersey Docks and Harbour Board, for example, with its 'Grand Staircase' of Dumfries granite, panelled with Italian marble, its furnishings of Danzig Oak and Spanish mahogany, every door with its fittings of bronze, was a temple fit for world-wide commerce, no less; a show case for a great commercial city. In it my father took his place as Principal of the City College of Commerce, designed to train the regiment of white-collared workers required by the carrier industry. On the side, he advised merchants as to the state of the cotton crop, a subject on which he was an expert.

Entranced by the sights and sounds and smells of the dockside areas, I prowled the streets, peering into pawnshop windows full of seamen's gear, nipping smartly past the astonishingly ostentatious glories of the public houses, nervously exploring the curiously secretive Chinatown. Map-minded, as befitted a pupil of the Oxford woman graduate who had taught me geography at school, it was immediately evident that the heart of this town was the Pool that gave it its name. Some smart developer had spotted the potential of building a dock where ships could be repaired, since the River offered no safe anchorage. That shrewd stroke of foresight had turned the obscure settlement on the Mersey marshes into a viable port. Whereupon a very snug little society had quickly developed. When I first knew it, much of that old town still stood, though in a state of sad decrepitude. If only we had it now, what a tourist attraction it could be, for all the world like a pantomime set for Dick Whittington. Wide streets of Hanoverian houses—one actually called Hanover Street—fanned out from where the Pool had once been (with accommodation for the storage of merchandise alongside), flights of steps up to heavy front doors with lion-head knockers, and, here and there, long windows on the top floor running the width of the frontage to provide light for workpeople such as watchmakers and ribbon weavers. The model was essentially genteel. Not for the Liverpool Gentleman the rough contacts between master and man on the factory floor. Of the shaming trade which was an essential link in the carriage of goods, no trace remained except on the river frontage called the Goree where a few heavy manacles still hung in the wind (mistakenly believed by us to have served as shackles for recalcitrant slaves).

It had glumly been prophesied that the ending of the slave trade would see grass growing in the streets of Liverpool (not for nothing had I written essays at school on the abolition of slavery). The town itself was proof of how far otherwise had been the reality. Napoleon had helped by frightening shipping away from Bristol and the Channel ports. The mechanism of the slave trade had been easily adapted to the transport of the increasing tide of migrants who sought to escape from the Old World to the New. And, by the happiest of good fortune, Liverpool found itself ideally situated to act as keeper of the gates through which surged the flood-tide of the carrier trade between the 'dark satanic mills' (about which we had sung every Friday at school prayers), and the outer reaches of the British Empire.

I had only to look about me as I explored the entrancing scene to realise the melodrama of what happened next. Up the River's banks and down had spread dock after dock, warehouse after warehouse; massive behind strong walls, power personified. The Students' Union at the University shook with the rumble of trains in the Edge Hill tunnel beneath it, on their way to the whole spread of Lancashire. Long-boats with mysterious loads made their way along the dark and dirty water of the Leeds and Liverpool Canal over which our morning train rattled into town. The Banks, the Exchanges, the insurance offices designed to look like Venetian palaces or French chateaux, these stood for the world of big business, big inter-national business. It was to meet the needs of that world, the world of the great British Empire, that the town owed its existence. It was to the Empire that men looked for fame and fortune. This was never England!

Indubitably, then, a Boom City, a City of Change and Challenge, as our public relations people later put it. Muscle power on a vast scale was what was needed if the demand for ships and docks and railways was to be met and their loads man-handled on their way to and from foreign parts. The insatiable demand for labour created a vacuum into which was sucked an endless variety of people from an infinite variety of places and countries. Many never intended to stay. Bound for the New World, they paused to take whatever work they could, only to find themselves trapped in an inescapable cycle of poverty and squalor. Ignorant, without resources, driven by want, their determination to survive was the major gift they brought to the city of their reluctant adoption. What a gift it has proved to be!

The literal consequences were writ large in the sticks and stones all about me. Sheer pressure of numbers at the centre had quite evidently driven the better-off up and out, up to the rising ground behind the town, then out in ever-widening circles of suburban territory like Waterloo (where I myself now lived). Into the houses they vacated crowded the masses of the labouring class, creating conditions of such exceptional squalor that the town was driven to attack them with exceptional zeal and, in so doing, earned an enviable reputation as a pioneer in public health. (Even so, the last of the ill-famed courts were only cleared after a fine row with the conservationists in the 1980s. Here and there you can still discover back-to-backs, all tarted up now as glossy offices for medics and architects.) And when even that was not enough, street after street after street of rows of little Welsh red brick houses were hurriedly rushed up, all jammed together within easy reach of the docks. Like oil and water the uncongenial classes separated themselves out.

Long afterwards I discovered that Eleanor Rathbone, as a student down from Oxford, had remarked that what had come into existence out of nowhere was 'an extremely peculiar' society (M. D. Stocks, *Eleanor Rathbone*, London, Gollancz, 1949, p. 45), unique in its peculiarity. This was no cosy old-established human settlement which had suddenly undergone a late development, no community held together by shared memories and traditions, but a sprawling mass of strangers. Visiting celebrities cry out that it's not the place, it's the people that endow Liverpool with its character. How right they are. As a shy girl student, I quickly learned that a useful opening gambit on meeting strangers was to ask where they were from. The answer almost invariably was that, though they themselves were Liverpool born, their parents came from elsewhere. 'I'm a mixture of Scots and Welsh', or wherever, they would quite happily proclaim—unless, of course, one parent was of a different colour.

Not a society, then, but a conglomerate of ex-patriates in a foreign land. Thrown into the melting pot of a boom city, each clung nostalgically to the way of life of their homeland in a desperate effort to assert their individuality against the pressures of a mass society. A local doctor commented that the virtual imprisonment in squalor of so great a number of people over so long a period constituted an experiment in Darwinism. 'The surviving character was a product of unnatural selection' (Dr Leslie Mackenzie, *Liverpool Daily Post*, 18 May 1913). It is a legacy which is still with us and one to which much of the city's contemporary character owes its origin. As late as the 1970s, a commentator could still remark that 'one of the great obstacles to communication in the Merseyside area is the feud mentality' (Gillian Reynolds, *Arts Alive*, June 1972)—this even before the elevation of football pitches into battle grounds.

There was no prospect here of any meshing together of the lily-fingered and the horny-handed. The River demanded both but never the twain could become one. It was this disproportion of chronically poor and illiterate people, whose constant renewal hopelessly overloaded the social structure, that gave rise to that continuing succession of problems of urban adjustment and social education which dog Liverpool to this day.

It was a while before it dawned on me that I was myself a migrant, displaying all the characteristics I so patronisingly observed in others. My father was one of the sons of a farthing grocer on Glasgow Green, himself a migrant to the city from the farmlands of Perthshire. Like all his brothers, he worked his way through University on the traditional bag of meal but, prospects being poor in Scotland, was compelled to seek his livelihood elsewhere. Hence, after a spell in the colonial hierarchy of Egypt, our eventual arrival in Liverpool. There was no question of our doing as Rome did now that we lived here. Even at the age of 90, my mother still referred to Scotland when she used the word 'home', still refused to do even the most urgent of sewing, or to allow the playing of cards, on a Sunday. So my home was Scottish but I lived in England. I learned to be bilingual, able to talk fluently in 'BBC' to the world at large but lapsing into lowland Scots when I was in family company. We clung to our origins, our lives centred in the Presbyterian church, with no other connection with the wider community. Indeed a typical Liverpudlian.

I can only marvel now that it never seemed to occur to me in my early days that the coin of the city's success had another side, and a singularly unlovely one at that. When we went to town, the overhead railway took us through a panorama of dockside streets, the whole length of the riverside from Bootle to the Pier Head—close packed bricks and mortar, visibly squalid with poverty of mind and body. The pubs, the pawnshops, the backyards full of clutter, the hutch-like outside lavatories; acres and acres of it. No gentility here, only gaunt Catholic churches and the great barracks of School Board schools set in asphalt play-grounds. None of that meant anything to me. A public school education wasn't intended to be a ground for the cultivation of compassion. Poverty passed me by. I had never myself tasted it. I felt no guilt, no anger, no pity. To me, the poor were the stuff of literature or painting, romance and drama, barefoot actors on the stage of history.

Yet, curiously, one quite other recollection stands out sharply from the background of my first impressions.

I still remember standing at the foot of the stair-case, the very first night I arrived, saying goodnight to my father. They weren't the sort of stairs we had had in our previous houses, which were just a means of getting from one floor to another. These swept up in wide and shallow steps, curving round the hallway with a kind of amplitude that made them a feature and not just a necessity. Father asked me if I liked the house and I, all unaware of what I was saying, replied 'I never thought *we* would live in a house like this'.

It is only now that I understand that what I was experiencing was the dawn of an awareness (on my part) that the ramifications of my life extended far beyond family and school. There were people like us who led good upright Glaswegian lives. There were the poor, a species apart, who lived lives of squalor. And now I realised that there were 'Them'; unidentifiable beings: somehow superior, somehow threatening, who lived lives of ease in houses like the one in which I now found myself. Waterloo wasn't high-tea territory as Ealing had been. People who lived in houses like these wouldn't eat their dinners at mid-day as we had always done. (Mother and father quarrelled over that for years to come; the minute father was away from home, we reverted to high-tea.) At that stage it completely passed me by that the sharp division of a society into separate classes was something that could not, and must not, be tolerated. Yet it must have been then that the seeds were sown that were to bear a crop of total commitment to the fight against the injustice of a social system based on discrimination.

There I might well have remained, stuck fast in a haze of romanticism, but for the fact that my father, being an admirably progressive sort of person, had always assumed that I, as well as my brothers, would go to a University. He did his best to persuade me to apply to Oxford but the prissiness of their rules and regulations repelled me. (When I innocently remarked at my interview at one College that my brother was already at Exeter College and so would be able to visit me, I was smartly trounced on the ground that men visitors were not permitted; how would they know that he was really my brother?!) Instead, I embarked on a degree course at Liverpool, choosing geography for no other reason than that it seemed the most likely to have any relevance to my fascination with the city.

I had, at that stage, no great sense of purpose, shying away from the probability that, at the end of the road, I would find myself a teacher. I was immature and dumb, a typical girls' grammar school product of the day; groomed to imbibe knowledge without argument. The days passed pleasantly enough, enlivened only by such mildly subversive behaviour as the raising of money to buy an alarm clock for a particularly long-winded young lecturer.

Yet for all that I was quite content, I instantly abandoned geography when, in 1923, I read in the local paper of the appointment of a Professor of Social Science at the University and of his intention to set up a course for the study of social institutions. I knew at once that this was the place for me. Ever since I had come to Liverpool my imagination had been tantalised by my longing to comprehend the goings-on of this great ant-heap of a city. Here was my opportunity. But secretly, hidden deep down beyond my own comprehension, was my desperate need to come to terms with the turmoil of the perpetual conflict between my parents. Mother so loyal to her Lowland Scots tradition, father eager and ambitious to move into the cosmopolitan world of twentieth century Liverpool; the pair of them incessantly locked in conflict. And me, struggling with a passionate in-built need for self-assertion that left me baffled and ashamed: where did I fit in?

Without even consulting my parents, who, after all, would have to pay my fees, I switched courses and headed off in this new direction. And in doing so, I blundered slap onto the middle of the stage on which the mighty drama of the Rise and Fall of the Welfare State was already under way.

Chapter 2
THE CREED OF SOCIAL RESPONSIBILITY

In which I describe how the turn of the century saw the coming
together in Liverpool of the moral commitment of the merchant
community, the idealism of the young University and the passion
of the women's demand for equal citizenship. The outcome was an
Urban Ideal, based on the principle of the universal right to social
responsibility as an attribute of citizenship.

I set off for the University in 1923, my pigtails coiled over my ears like head-
phones (as was the fashion of the day). The significance of what I was doing
completely escaped me. It simply never occurred to me to ask questions about
how the University came to exist in what was, at that time, the improbable
setting of a commercial city. Nor how I as a young woman came to be there,
all set to acquire a degree with a view to embarking on an independent career
of my own. It is only now I realise that I was the unsuspecting beneficiary of a
most remarkable coming-together of the right people, in the right place, at
the right time. Without the solid base of the moral commitment of Liverpool's
philanthropic tradition, the University would never have come into being.
Without the University, that commitment would never have blossomed into
the magical vision of the urban city as the finest flower of the Industrial Revolution. Without the stimulus and the opportunity offered by these two together, the passionate hunger of women to play their part in the society in
which they found themselves might well have run into the sands of frustration. And, without the goad of the desperate necessity of the great mass of
poverty, the inventive and idealistic programme of social reform devised in
those early years would never have come to fruition.

Trying to think back to my early days at the University, what is vivid in my
memory is the impact made on me by G. S. Veitch, the Professor of History.
Veitch was a local product, born and bred, and his recent appointment over

the head of a respected Oxford rival had caused considerable fuss. He was a type-cast stage professor, totally entranced by local history, which he saw it to be his privilege and duty to teach us. It was thanks to Veitch that I began to comprehend Liverpool as a city, a growing, changing entity; not static but with a vitality and life of its own. Urbanology was the word he used for it.

As students, we were blandly indifferent to our obligations to our founders, regarding their claim to civic virtue with cynicism. Resenting any comparison with Oxford, we yet derided what we dubbed the public-lavatory style of the building they had provided for us. We regarded their success at making money as somehow despicable. We deplored their ability to turn a blind eye on the fact that the wealth that paid for their benefactions had derived from the drink-sodden poor and the unmentionable slave trade. We mocked the choice of 'For advancement of learning and ennoblement of life' as the University's motto. Eyeing the vast workhouse across the road from the University, it was obvious even to me, as a callow student, that life in Liverpool could certainly do with a bit of ennobling. How very typical of the twenties we must have been and what a lot we had to learn.

It was only years later, when the boredom of suburban life drove me to write my book on *Charitable Effort in Liverpool in the Nineteenth Century* (Liverpool, Liverpool University Press, 1951, reprinted as *Charity Rediscovered*, 1992), that I realised that extravagant expressions of civic pride concealed an alternative philanthropy which was to make as vital a contribution to the city's well-being as did any art gallery or library. This originated with the small community of non-conformists who found scope in the 'boom city' that was Liverpool denied them elsewhere. On the basis of that blend of moral principle and sound business sense, characteristic of their kind, they had throughout the previous century explored the application of charitable principles to the contemporary problem of poverty. Slowly, they arrived at the conclusion that poverty was not an act of God but a social disease for which the remedy must lie in 'physical' rather than 'spiritual' civilisation. It was the sustained endeavour to put this into practice that had earned for the city its proud record of 'Liverpool Firsts'—in the provision of environmental improvements—which were so very unlike the good works of Victorian tradition.

Outstanding amongst this group was William Rathbone, father of the Miss Rathbone who towered above our lives as students. Confronted by the unprecedented squalor of contemporary Liverpool, his reaction was to apply to the problem of poverty the good business sense that governed his daily life. 'What ought to be done, can be done', was his maxim; the only point open to argument was how best to do it. Typically, when he wrote a little book on *Social*

Duties (By a Man of Business, London, Macmillan, 1867) his own preference for its title had been *Method versus Muddle and Waste in Charitable Effort*. He was surely the first to apply a performance indicator to philanthropy when he proposed that 10% of income should be the target for charitable giving. His example, and that of others in the Unitarian Church to which he belonged, won universal approbation to which their enviable wealth no doubt contributed. (Though, on occasion, the reaction was one of resentment against such a surfeit of moral rectitude: Josephine Butler had some sharp things to say about the attitude of her suburban neighbours in Sefton Park to her campaign against the Contagious Diseases Act and Mary Macaulay flatly refused to set up house in Liverpool on her marriage to Charles Booth.)

William Rathbone's long crusade for higher education reached its climax in 1903 with the granting of a charter to the University. The remarkable contribution made to the life of the city (not least in regard to its tremendous burden of social need), by members of the University staff who not only shared his vision, but extended it far and away beyond his expectations, is a forgotten chapter of Liverpool history.

The idea of making provision for higher education originated with the little group of Unitarians who lived around Sefton Park. Being dissenters, they had become acutely aware of the lack of opportunities for the education of their sons, and even more their daughters, either locally or elsewhere. Proud of their city—Liverpool was the wealthiest in the country after London—they determined on founding their own university though the original modest intention was for no more than a college.

His daughter Eleanor's description of William Rathbone's shrewd grasp of how to promote the proposed college could go straight into a modern manual of community development. He and his colleagues decided that not an unnecessary penny should be spent on buildings until a sufficient staff of professors and lecturers had been adequately endowed.

> Get the right men and let them prove their worth and then plenty of Liverpool citizens will come forward to provide them with all the equipment they want. (E. F. Rathbone, *William Rathbone*, London, Macmillan, 1905, p. 337)

Equally shrewd was the decision to secure the endowment of Chairs in subjects relevant to local industries, rather than those of academic tradition. The policy was sound: trust a Rathbone for that. What started out as 'little more than a University extension centre, a fashionable night school, with an endowed staff and a few day classes', became an established local institution in a remarkably short time. 'Once planted, how it flowers into achievement' ex-claimed one of its earliest professors in delighted surprise (J. M. Mackay, *A New University*, Liverpool, Liverpool University Press, 1914, p. 10).

Whether by chance or as a consequence of Rathbone's happy knack of re-cognising a tide when it flowed in his favour, there was an additional ingre-dient in the situation which proved decisive in forming the character of the new establishment. This was the fact that the decision to go for able men, rather than showy buildings, was matched by a movement in the university world in general for academics to seek careers in the raw institutions of the North rather than in the establishments of academic tradition.

> The staff of University College when I first knew it consisted largely of young men, chosen with such warrant of ability as was obtainable, inter-ested not so much to carry on University education in the North (for the thing was new) as to invent it. (Sir Walter Raleigh, *A Miscellany*, Liver-pool, Liverpool University Press, 1914, p. 2)

Why so many of these young men should have been Scots is a matter for speculation. Certainly many were influenced by Patrick Geddes who, from his Outlook Tower in Edinburgh, brought about a new awareness of the po-tential of urban living: he is said to have invented the word conurbation (Paddy Kitchen, *A Most Unsettling Person*, London, Gollancz, 1975).

Equally far-reaching was the drive in Scottish university circles to relate moral philosophy, then a basic subject, more closely to real life. The key figure in this was Edward Caird, Professor of Moral Philosophy at Glasgow University (H. Jones and J. Muirsheald, *Life and Philosophy of Edward Caird*, Glas-gow, Maclehose Jackson, 1921).

Caird's argument was that membership of a civilised society must necessa-rily 'confer on every man the right and impose on every man the duty' to strive after fulfilment; every man being, of course, a generic term which included women. This was generally accepted in principle, but Caird took it much further by emphasising that this implied the existence of a society in which the principle would be viable in practice. Hence his important conclusion that the duty and the right to work towards the creation of such a society must be accepted as a universal attribute of citizenship.

Whatever its inspiration, the characteristic blend of applied idealism came to dominate the development of the young College. The records of the early years shine with an astonishing sense of missionary zeal. Amongst them the Arts Faculty was outstanding, undoubtedly inspired by the magnetism of the first Professor of History, once described as 'that formidable Highlander'.

John Mackay was a Scot of the Carlyle breed: prophet, priest and king to the group which gathered round him, and came to be known as the 'New Testament' (see Thomas Kelly, *For Advancement of Learning*, Liverpool, Liverpool University Press, 1981). An eccentric of dominating character, the subject of awed reminiscence for the rest of their lives amongst those who encountered him, the doctrine he so passionately preached was that they:

> were assisting at the birth of a new type of University in England and that to that type of University belonged the future. (*A Miscellany*, op. cit.)

He was wholly convinced that out of the mutual exchange between responsible business men and inspired academics would come a way of life as yet undreamed of; combining, in one glorious unity, the vigour and the progressive outlook of an industrial society with the principles of eternal truth and beauty for which a University stood.

> Through its university, Liverpool was to be a new Athens, saving the country from its materialism by the clearness of its thought, the fineness of its ideals and even the beauty of its buildings ... It was grand to listen and to hope and even to believe. (C. H. Reilly, *Scaffolding in the Sky*, London, Routledge, 1938, p.7)

Reading the records of the time, the old magic stirs again. These men had a vision, they saw themselves as missionaries but they were no do-gooders. Levellers certainly, but their purpose was to level upwards, to the highest standards imaginable, the quality of life of the whole society. And it was a vision that was rooted literally in reality.

> The college was set on a hill, flanked by slaughter-houses, supported by the workhouse, edged by a gaping railway tunnel, surrounded by mean streets. No haunts of ancient peace for sanctuary. No groves for academic calm. Only the belching roar of trains for organ-music, with the savour of fried fish for incense at the alter of his prayers. (*A Miscellany*, op. cit., p. 82)

The young incomers took over as their campus the adjacent squares and terraces of the previous century which were in course of being evacuated by the drift to the suburbs of the merchant families who built them. Partly to raise support for the College, but even more on principle, they immersed themselves in the affairs of the city. They gave lectures on anything and everything to anybody who would listen. They served on public bodies. They intervened in local politics. Ramsay Muir, the sprightly Professor of Modern History, single-handedly kept up a newspaper correspondence by writing letters to an editor under eleven different names, in eleven different styles, in order to provoke interest in some project dear to his heart.

Their promotion of the study and practice of drama, painting and all the current forms of applied art was a spectacular demonstration of practising what they preached. The presence in their midst of artists of the calibre and character of Augustus John and Charles Reilly brought leaven to the somewhat ponderous display of affluent wealth exemplified by the leaders of the commercial community. The University staff, it was said, sparkled like ornaments on a Christmas tree. They painted their ceilings in strange colours when all about them stuck to white. They hung their walls with scarlet silk and filled their rooms with art nouveau furniture. I still remember struggling to conceal my astonishment on seeing the murals which decorated a Professor's flat in Bedford Street: could they have been the work of Augustus John? They established folk dancing (from which I was to benefit twenty years on) and studied Gypsy lore. They inspired a School of Architecture and a Repertory Theatre. Together, they originated the tradition of artistic vitality which characteristics the city to this day.

There was, however, much more to the University's intention than merely disturbing the complacency of the local community. Underneath the superficial gaieties ran a current of the most profound seriousness. For it was essential to their philosophy that just as 'art' must be related to 'reality' so academic standards and training must be applied, right across the board, to subjects never before taught in establishments of higher education. The end product was an infusion of fresh thinking into every aspect of the city's existence, and the bold application of original theories to its practical problems (whatever their nature).

This was nowhere more evident than in the approach to the baffling social problems of the day. By putting the ideal of the good life firmly into the centre of the picture, as the prime aim and attribute of urban citizenship, the whole problem of poverty was set in an entirely new context. And, by opening the doors of their splendiferous red-brick building to middle class women hungry for education, they introduced into the situation a totally new input of incalculable importance.

It is no exaggeration to claim that it was the impact of the women's movement that vitalised what might otherwise have been no more than a medley of high-flown ambitions into a practical and energetic programme of social reform. Nor can it be denied that, amongst that generation of out-standing daughters of the merchant philanthropists, Eleanor Rathbone played the leading part.

It is significant that the outstanding figure on the drive for social reform in Liverpool at that time should have been a woman. As a Rathbone born and bred, a philosopher by training and a leader of women, Eleanor Rathbone was a one-person demonstration of the synthesis of principle and practice—the vital process whereby moral sensibility and social circumstance acted and reacted upon each other to produce a practical solution—that came to constitute the magic of the Liverpool approach to social reform.

The facts of Eleanor's life are characteristically straightforward. She was born in 1872 in the London house used as a base by her father during his long service as a local Member of Parliament, a rare Liberal in a consistently Tory stronghold. The real focus for family life was, however, in Liverpool at Greenbank, the pleasant house which had originally been acquired as a summer retreat (later to become a university clubhouse). Compared with the examination-ridden adolescence of today, Eleanor's growing-up appears to be perhaps more enviable than it really was. Formal education was minimal. In its place was the opportunity to meet the many interesting and important people who sought her parents' company, and to observe at close quarters, in their example and that of her father and mother, the practical application of moral principles to daily living.

Remarkably for one of her sex and generation, she eventually went to Oxford to study philosophy. Her father's enthusiasm for the higher education of women could hardly have failed to influence her. At the presentation of an illuminated address to the Principal of University College on the occasion of his marriage, he is reported to have

> expressed his satisfaction at seeing so many ladies who for the first time were enjoying the benefits of a real University education. This had been the aim of his life, and he had lived to see it completed ... The sight of that large room thronged with happy looking students of both sexes made him feel as happy as on any day of his life. The orchestra then played a series of popular airs and the evening was brought to a close by guests and hosts singing together Auld Lang Syne. (*University College Magazine*, Vol. 3, 1887)

It is worth noting that her contemporaries at Somerville were impressed by the fierceness of her feminism. This cannot be attributed to any inequality in the way she was treated at home, but may well have reflected resentment against that element of complacency in Liverpool society which so bitterly impressed itself, in turn, upon Josephine Butler and Charles Booth's wife, Mary Macaulay.

On her return home in 1896, there was, of course, no thought of earning her own living: had she been a son, she would presumably have embarked upon a career as a merchant. As it was, she was singularly fortunate in that the companionship of her ageing father constituted for her a quite exceptional apprenticeship in public service. She quickly became involved in local affairs, becoming a District Visitor on behalf of the Central Relief Society (the organisation instituted by her father to introduce method into the muddle of relief-giving). She was also a Manager of Granby Street Board School, and inevitably, secretary of the Liverpool Women's Industrial Council set up to direct public attention to the unsatisfactory conditions under which women were often employed.

The bitter reality of poverty in Liverpool, as she now encountered it, profoundly disturbed her. Confronted by 'a world with all its wrongs shouting in one's ears and every miserable face claiming kinship' (Stocks, op. cit., p. 53), her awareness of 'unsuspected obligations' became so acute as on occasion to amount to almost literal pain. Neither the philosophical habits of thought she had acquired at Oxford, nor the benevolent philanthropy of the merchant community in which she now found herself, provided her with an adequate answer. The social reform that was obviously urgently needed would require a much more radical approach.

Little trace remains of what part Eleanor played in the activities of the academic community. Knowing her, I doubt if she fitted easily into the more light-hearted goings-on of the artistic set. Her own house in Penny Lane, where, as one of her 'apprentice' politicians, I used to attend drawing-room meetings about the suffrage movement, was essentially conventional, complete with parlour maid. Nevertheless, given the Greenbank tradition of hospitality, and the out-going style of the New Testament group, she must have had every opportunity of participating in the running debate about the whole issue of the development of a more scientific approach to social policy. She was a member of the Economic and Statistical Society: the first-hand knowledge that she was able to feed into their discussions must have been a welcome counter to any tendency to flights of fancy on the part of the academics. More importantly, it was through her association with the Victoria Women's Settlement that the partnership between town and gown came to be invigorated by the passion of the women's movement.

The Victoria Settlement had been opened in 1898, its original aim being 'to plant in a centre of vice, squalor and misery, a little oasis of education, refinement and sympathy' (*Charitable Effort*, op. cit., p. 141.]. Eleanor joined the committee at the point where the difficulty of finding from amongst the sheltered daughters of the local families a volunteer capable of managing the project, together with the growing pressure for a more scientific approach to the relief of poverty, eventually persuaded the committee to look further afield for a professional Warden. Elizabeth Macadam was duly appointed in 1903.

The daughter of a Scottish minister who was said to have taken to drink, it was rumoured that Elizabeth Macadam took up social work because her fiancé first seduced and then married her aunt's housemaid. More relevantly, she had acquired at the Women's University Settlement in London a firm grasp of the purpose for which a Settlement should exist: to provide an opportunity for:

> serious, thoughtful and organised effort to tackle social ills not only as part of personal religion, but as a social obligation. (Elizabeth Macadam, *The Social Servant in the Making*, London, Allen & Unwin, 1945, p. 22)

By the most fortunate of chances, the arrival of the new Warden coincided with Eleanor Rathbone's personal liberation from domestic responsibilities following the death of her father in 1902.

The close friendship and powerful working partnership which developed between the two women was to last for the rest of their lives. Eleanor's philosophical flair for establishing the principles of any matter was complemented by Elizabeth's Scottish practicality. Their physical stamina became legendary; it was matched by the persistent quality of the determination with which they pursued their chosen ends—in particular, their indestructible vision of the part women could and should play in public affairs.

As those of us who knew them in their later years could well imagine, the impact of the two women on the Settlement's affairs was immediate. The original little house was abandoned in favour of much more substantial premises nearby (where I myself served my apprenticeship and which continued in use until quite recently). A drive on influential friends, of whom they had many, put the work on a sound financial basis. Most importantly, the purpose of the project was crisply redefined:

> .. the double purpose .. (is) first, to bring the lives of the two classes vaguely called 'rich and poor' into more natural and more friendly relationships with each other, and secondly, to further the more thorough and scientific study and treatment of the problem of poverty. (*Annual Report*, 1903)

The change of direction could not have come at a better time. The first disturbing effects of improved education for girls were just beginning to make themselves felt. The more progressive of the leading local families had taken to sending their daughters to Cheltenham Ladies College, or the Belvedere School in Liverpool (a Girls' Public Day School Trust school), an experience which returned the girls to their homes with active minds and heightened social sensibilities. The contrast between the stimulus of school, and what appears to have been the singularly ponderous social life of Liverpool's commercial classes, was presumably hard to bear. The Victoria Settlement provided a welcome escape, all the more so because of the unquestionable respectability of its new management. Numbers increased rapidly.

Though the companionship offered by the Settlement to frustrated young women from the suburbs was enjoyable, the standards set for voluntary workers was demanding. On Eleanor's insistence, careful records were kept of every activity, with a view to providing a body of reliable information on which proposals for reform might be founded. In addition, special inquiries were undertaken such as that carried out at the request of the Royal Commission on the Poor Law (which consisted of evidence from over one hundred widows of dock workers). These inquiries were carefully modelled on the methods worked out by Charles Booth; the gift of a complete set of the seventeen volumes of his own great survey of the *Life and Labour of the People of London* is recorded in an early Annual Report. Papers were prepared by various workers for presentation to the local Economic and Statistical Society (of which Eleanor was a founder member). The opening paper in the *Transactions of the Economic and Statistical Society* for 1906, for example, was a report by a Miss Phelps entitled 'An Enquiry in Connection with Underfed School Children'. It concluded with the bold claim that:

> Too much value cannot be attached to investigations of this kind. They alone can afford the necessary basis for sound economic and social arguments, and correct the errors so often evident in the attempts to apply the conclusions of purely abstract theory to existing conditions.

The overall strategy was not so much to start up novel projects, as to provide a corps of trained women who would take advantage of any openings which might come their way. There was a degree of participation by voluntary workers in local government services which they were quick to seize and which we today must regard with envy. The inquiry into the feeding of school children was, for example, tied in with service as school managers as a way into the controversy over whether the Local Authority should exercise its powers to provide free school meals. Again, information collected as to the prevalence of unemployment amongst local women led to an active interest in the work of Evening Continuation Schools and to attempts to form some sort of Union which would represent the urgent need of women and girls for employment. Three Settlement workers, one of them Eleanor herself, actually attempted to promote a strike. In a Paper to the Economic and Statistical Society (published in the *Transactions* for 1907), they reported that:

> we tried to ferment a rebellion among a little knot of eight workers against an exaction which we and they considered unfair. After much talking, we thought we had got them to the point of sending a deputation of protest to the employer, but eventually three or four of those who had seemed hottest backed out, and the others explained apologetically, and as we knew truly, that it was because these women had nothing at all to depend on but their work and did not dare to risk offending the firm.

It was quickly obvious that whatever the objective might be, be it an attack on the problems of chronic poverty, the introduction of methodical giving into the chaos of charitable effort, or the need to find occupation for middle-class women, spontaneous action by well-meaning amateurs could do little but harm. Intervention in the affairs of other human beings could only be justified on the basis of carefully considered principles. Every worker must be trained.

Talk of the need for training for women wishing to become social workers, as distinct from charitable volunteers, had been in the air for some time: Eleanor spoke disparagingly of the amateur District Visitors she encountered in the Central Relief Society. The only available qualification that was in any way relevant, was that of Lady Sanitary Inspector (started by an enterprising local Medical Officer of Health who was prepared to offer employment in his Department to those who took the course) (E. W. Hope, *Health at the Gateway*, Cambridge, Cambridge University Press, 1931). The idea that the universities should enter this field is said to have originated in the mind of C. S. Loch, Secretary of the London Council of Social Service and, subsequently, author of the Majority Report of the Royal Commission on the Poor Law (op. cit., p. 13). Certainly it was through him that the indefatigable Edward Gonner, Professor of Economics, heard of the arrival of the high-powered Macadam at the Victoria Settlement.

His approach was received with enthusiasm. It was, however, an enthusiasm which was by no means commonly shared. The New Testament group could be relied on to fight the battle against those who rejected the proposition that social work should find a place in the academic curriculum, but opposition from the charitable public was, as Macadam recollected long afterwards, considerable.

> The practical bodies had genuine and not altogether ill-founded fears that the universities were not in a position to supply the experience which they considered essential. They feared that classroom study would 'choke out the real thing', the human approach; they feared that training removed from the centres of activity to the cloistered atmosphere of the university would inevitably become less applied and realist in its bearings. Employing bodies and committees at the beginning of the century were much less tempted by the lure of university degrees than they are today. They looked for solid qualities such as capacity for hard work, technical efficiency, tact, a sense of vocation or missionary spirit (an essential quality especially in the eyes of those who offered small salaries) which are not necessarily the product of the lecture room. (*The Social Servant in the Making*, op. cit., p. 33)

But, though the opposition appeared to be intractable, it was as nothing when confronted by the intensity of the demand which emanated from the Settlement. A contemporary photograph of Eleanor presents a picture for which formidable is the only possible adjective; with a hard straw hat skewered to the head and a set of the jaw which must have intimidated every opponent especially bearing in mind the aura of prestige which inevitably surrounded a member of her family. Elizabeth Macadam must have been equally alarming, though in a different way, representing as she did the first of that new breed of women—the professional social worker—whose salaried status endowed her with an independence which few could previously have encountered in a young female.

No time was lost. Within a matter of months of their first meeting, the scheme for what was called the School of Social Science and Training for Social Work was ready. It was, wrote Elizabeth Macadam:

> the outcome of arrangements between the University of Liverpool, the Victoria Settlement for Women and the Liverpool Central Relief and Charity Organisation Society. (op. cit., p. 23)

The bald statement conceals a considerable massing of talents and pulling of strings in which Eleanor played her rôle.

To begin with, in January 1905, no more than periodic courses of lectures were provided, largely attended by voluntary workers and clergy, with a dozen students from the Settlement providing a nucleus. The lecturers, of whom Eleanor was one, were mainly volunteers from the University staff. The subject was new and the approach to its teaching often novel. Indeed, although the findings of Cyril Burt, for instance, lecturer in Experimental Psychology at the University, have subsequently been sharply challenged, at the time it was said of him that:

.. his practical classes were often exciting and included such things as hypnosis, and the detection of mock criminals in realistically staged situations. Among the students these demonstrations became affectionately known as 'Burt's music hall turns'. (*University Recorder*, November 1973)

The embryo School faced every kind of difficulty, both financial and because of hostility towards the teaching of social work as an academic discipline. The students were an awkward medley who were hard to teach; Ramsay Muir, Professor of History, protested against the presence in his class of ladies in white gloves. As for the small supporting committee, though their commitment was unshakeable, they were each forceful characters in their own right, not least the spiky Macadam, on whose goodwill the School depended for practical training opportunities.

However, no doubt thanks to their joint determination and, I suspect, Eleanor's financial support, the new School survived its difficult early days. With the appointment in 1906 of a hitherto unknown curate from a London parish as tutor organiser (of whom, more later), the School set about the forbidding task of defining in real terms what Beatrice Webb called the creed and craft of social work.

No record remains of the endless discussion and debate which developed in and around the School of Social Work, as it was first called. The 'New Testament' philosophy, as such, was never spelled out in so many words. As for Eleanor, she fought shy of any attempt to reduce her thoughts to paper, preferring (like so many of her generation) to seek refuge from the mental strife of trying to 'find answers to unanswerable questions' in strictly practical activity.

Happily, a commentary on the way the thinking of this little group of colleagues developed is available in the shape of a book by the Professor of Philosophy; John MacCunn, yet another Scot, was one of the most convinced and most convincing of the 'New Testament' group. In 1911 he published, under the title of *Liverpool Addresses on Ethics of Social Work* (Liverpool, Liverpool University Press), a series of lectures he had given to a variety of audiences from 1901 onwards from which the following quotations are selected. It is a dull enough book to look at, with its dated format, and dull enough to read with its period formality. For all that, what he has to say still glows with the passionate interest and conviction with which this band of pioneers explored the new territory which lay before them. What emerged out of the give and take between town and gown, between theory and practice, between ideal and reality, was that blend of moral principle, hard fact, and visionary zeal which was to become uniquely characteristic of the Liverpool contribution to social reform.

It is evident that what MacCunn presented was an amalgam of the thinking of the whole group. Their starting point was the bitter paradox with which MacCunn's hearers must have been all too wearily familiar: that, in spite of the mass and variety of effort that went into ameliorating what was called the 'condition of the people', nevertheless the problem of poverty in the midst of great wealth was rapidly becoming a built-in feature of urban life. 'With social vitality—it is too true a tale—comes social disease' (ibid.). Poverty as a way of life had become a problem in its own right and one quite distinct from the relief of individual distress. They must face up to the fact of 'the collapse of the bygone fool's paradise that the health of the social organism can be left to take care of itself'. Inspired by the vision of the good life, as expounded by the 'New Testament', MacCunn declared that:

> all will never be well with our country until its citizens, and as many of them as possible, pass far beyond the narrow pale of private interests and make the public good, in one or other of its manifold departments, their deliberate, conscious and direct aim. (ibid.)

Seen in this light, that anyone, however mean, should live a life of poverty and squalor, became no less than an offence against their dignity as citizens, a wicked waste of the glorious opportunities of life in an urban society, a hindrance and an obstruction to the progress of the community as a whole. What was called for was:

> the transformation of the compassionate relief of suffering and the righting of wrongs into a settled resolve to emancipate their fellow citizens

from the manifold obstructions of vice, disease, poverty, ignorance, thoughtlessness, which in diabolical alliance baffle the forward-struggling strivings of the human spirit. (ibid.)

The duty to emancipate; this was the theme underlying all that followed. How the words must have struck home to the hearts of women! But how was this to be done? It was not enough to love the city; they must also understand it. And if the desire to meddle—as meddle they must—with the complex delicately-balanced vulnerable social organism was not to do more harm than good, then they must make sure that they knew what they were doing. In other words, 'social work must rest on social science' (ibid.).

Had MacCunn spoken only for the University group, all this might have amounted to no more than an enthusiasm for the development of the 'science of society' as an academic subject. But he went on to stress, with all the passion of which he was signally capable, the importance of a moral component as being essential to the process of social reform. The study of social problems and the drive for their solution must, he insisted over and over again, have its origins in, and derive its inspiration from, a profound and universal acceptance of social responsibility. 'Emotion without ideas may be blind and reckless, but ideas, however just and reasonable, without emotion are barren'. He was prepared to assume that people such as those who composed his audience would thus be motivated—why else would they be there?—but what of 'the democracy'?

.. if this is true, if in the programme of this and other like Schools a social conscience is essential to all who mean, whether as workers or researchers, to grapple with social problems, what, we may well ask, are we to expect of the democratic electorate who seem so eager to solve these same problems for themselves? Can we expect a man to work for social ends? (ibid.)

All very well to trumpet aloud the need for a dramatically 'vast expansion of the area of recognised social obligations' (ibid.) but in hard fact 'a social conscience is not a congenital endowment .. it needs all the agencies of evolution, from the family onwards, to secure its development' (ibid.). And to bring this about would be no easy task.

Easy and light .. would be the education of a people, if it were only a matter of popular enlightenment. The infinitely harder task is to capture

> the Will—especially the wayward and formidable Will of a great democracy—to capture the will and yoke it to the unselfish, resolute service of the public good. (ibid.)

Over and over again MacCunn returned to this question, confidently declaring that:

> the answer lay in the belief which may truly be said to lie at the roots of Western civilisation—the belief in the worth, the potential worth at any rate, of the individual life .. Has not charitable effort, in all its many modes, been bearing witness to it by insisting, full in the face of appearances, upon finding worth even in the 'worthless'? Has not democracy recognised it as at once root and fruit of reforming energy? (ibid.)

This was the fundamental principle upon which the whole edifice of social reform must be founded. 'Faith in the worth of men .. is the tap-root of social motive' (ibid.). Without it, no society could survive the ordeal of confrontation with degradation and squalor. With it, they would never lack inspiration and courage. 'Man has intelligence, therefore man is capable of more than "death in life"' (ibid.). Which, being interpreted, applied equally to women as to men.

This was undoubtedly a 'new testament' so far as social reform was concerned. The start and finish of it all was the astonishing declaration of the right of the individual to social responsibility as the essential and universal attribute of citizenship, astonishing and fundamental then as it still is today. This was indeed a recipe for social change.

So much, then, for the creed of social responsibility. But what of the craft? How to put the principle into practice? This was the question that was to dominate all the long years of the century that lay ahead.

Chapter 3
THE CRAFT OF SOCIAL RESPONSIBILITY

In which I describe the first steps towards the creation of a society wherein the principle of universal social responsibility would be viable. The age-old pursuit of individual betterment as the target of social reform gives way to the novel concept of the improvement of the quality of life of the community as a whole.

To arrive at the expression of a creed of universal social responsibility had called for moral courage of a high order; but to take the next step of implementing the duty to create a society wherein the principle would be viable, required imagination and determination of an equal intensity. The ultimate aim of the little group that propounded it was the creation of a Good Society, but they were totally in the dark as to how this was to be achieved. The improvement of the individual was an age-old topic, but the very idea of developing the quality of life of a community as the target of social reform was barely comprehensible—it was almost as a by-product that they laid down the guidelines of community development. These were pioneers, constant as to the direction in which they wanted to move, but with everything to learn about how to achieve their aim.

With all my experience as a politician, of persuading the human race to proceed along the road to social change, my mind boggles at the magnitude of the task these pioneers set themselves. As it is, I can only write as someone who heard about that early adventure into the unknown at first hand from the men and women who embarked upon it. At least I had the good fortune to come on the scene while many of them were still active in the pursuit of their vision of the Urban Ideal.

The gulf between the dream and the reality of the situation in the early years of the century must have been forbidding in the extreme. Poverty mounted daily. There were bread riots on Liverpool's St George's Plateau. In her Annual Report for 1908 Macadam wrote that:

> Most of us are perplexed and distressed at the beginning of this winter's work by the problems of unemployment and exceptional poverty which confront us. I think we must each feel our personal responsibility and must be prepared to make individual sacrifices, both of time and money. We must do all we can to understand the complicated conditions that lead to periods of distress, and how best to meet them, while at the same time we must throw our strength into whatever practical work we undertake, remembering we are working for the future as well as the present. (Victoria Settlement, *Annual Report*, October 1908)

What to do? Just as my own generation years later was to experience the exasperation of 'waiting for Seebohm' (*Report of the Committee on Local Authority and Allied Personal Services*, Cmnd. 3703, London, HMSO, 1968), so the long run-up to the publication of the Report of the Royal Commission on the Poor Law created a similar phoney stalemate where no one felt able to make a move. When the Report did eventually appear in February 1909, the airing by Sidney and Beatrice Webb of the underlying differences of opinion had been so extensive that its newsworthiness was greatly reduced, beyond astonishment at its sheer bulk. As the *Liverpool Courier* remarked on 15 February 1909 in a leading article headed 'Stones for Bread':

> As a result of three years' work, the Royal Commission has produced a document of portentous dimensions, the effect of which—so far as the majority's report is concerned—seems to be principally the suggestion of new names for old things.

Inevitably, attention focused on the break-up of the Poor Law. Indeed, some of the press reports totally ignored the implications of the proposed reforms so far as charitable work was concerned. Even the sharp-witted Beatrice Webb only introduced the topic of the relationship between the state and voluntary work into the subsequent campaign when she realised its value in securing support for the Minority Report (Beatrice Webb, *Our Partnership*, Cambridge, Cambridge University Press, 1915, p. 424). However, the speed with which Eleanor and her colleagues moved, to implement the recommendation that every large city should set up some form of voluntary aid council, makes it clear that considerable planning had taken place in Liverpool before ever the Report appeared. In the light of sub-sequent events, it is equally clear that a decisive contribution to that planning came from F. G. D'Aeth, the tutor at the School of Social Work.

Such crumbs of information as are available about the early life of Frederick

G. D'Aeth have so Wellsian a flavour that I am tempted to fill in the story for myself. He was born in 1875, his father a clerk in the Bank of England, his mother an unidentified Elizabeth Gosling. Somewhere along the line he changed his name from Death to D'Aeth but it is typical of his cultivated anonymity that he was always referred to by his initials and rarely by his first name. Two years as a non-collegiate student at St Stephen's House, Oxford, led to unhappy curacies in Burnley and Leytonstone. In a bitter article in his college magazine, which it is to their credit that they published, he warned prospective clergy of the unrewarding labour which would be theirs when they took up office.

No record is available to explain how a despairing curate in an obscure London parish found himself in charge of a highly experimental academic project in Liverpool, designed to test the possibility of training social workers at the University. He may well have known Elizabeth Macadam whilst she was at the London Women's University Settlement. It can only be assumed that his appointment resulted from the operations of that national network of reformers and intellectuals who served to disseminate the inspiration of men like Canon Barnett of Toynbee Hall in London. Certainly, as soon as D'Aeth arrived in Liverpool, he associated himself with the movement amongst Christian Union students for the setting up of what in 1906 became the University Settlement for men (to match that already available for women), himself serving as its first Honorary Warden.

> The Liverpool University Settlement, like Toynbee Hall, was founded by a small group sharing the belief that poverty was not an Act of God but a disease of the industrial system (Constance M. and Harold King, *The Two Nations*, Liverpool, Liverpool University Press, 1938, p. 6)

Following the common pattern of migrants to Liverpool, whatever his original intention, D'Aeth in fact settled there for life. His sister joined him, living at the Victoria Settlement. On his marriage to one of her friends, he moved into a house on the 'campus' in the terrace overlooking the site of the Anglican Cathedral (the foundations of which were then being laid). No doubt under his wife's influence, he became Chairman of the local branch of the English Folk Song and Dance Society (of which I myself, in due course, became a member).

By singular good fortune, when the Poor Law Report appeared in 1909, the current Lord Mayor (always a key figure in Liverpool's charitable scene), was Challoner Dowdall, a cousin of Eleanor's. Young, gifted, imaginative, with all the skills of the successful barrister, Dowdall brought the added zeal of a convert to the doctrine of the New Testament group, of which he was a member by virtue of his appointment to the staff of the progressive new Law Department at the University. Briefed by D'Aeth, no more brilliant an advocate of the need for the coordination of voluntary action could have been found. By a combination of personal charm and professional skill, he swept the highly individualistic cohorts of the charitable into agreeing that they would at least consider the idea of getting together to form a Council of Voluntary Aid (CVA). Before the opposition could firm up their opinions, he called a second Town Hall meeting, at which his audience was confronted with the results of a survey of what was going on under the guise of charity. This had been conducted by D'Aeth in his own free time, presumably with the assistance of the Victoria Settlement workers. To our survey-saturated society, this seems an obvious first step; but the idea of measuring a social situation was then both a strange and an intimidating innovation. In D'Aeth's skilled hands, it proved a decisive weapon.

There is no need to elaborate on the detail of what the Survey revealed. D'Aeth's report was unique only in that the chaos of effort which it uncovered was even worse than that familiar to most other cities; a reflection of the excessive zeal of the voluntary response in Liverpool. The press ranted melo-dramatically about the chaos of charity, the multiplicity of agencies, the mount-ing tide of need amongst the apparently chronic class of poor. D'Aeth's response was characteristically unemotional, to the point of being a positively boring understatement; a considerable achievement in the overheated atmo-sphere of the contemporary debate. There was, he mildly remarked, a tendency for agencies to be duplicated, or to overlap, thus involving a needless expendi-ture of time and money besides interfering with the efficiency of the work.

Faced with such a dismaying picture of confusion, the opposition wilted away. The combined talents of Dowdall and D'Aeth produced so skilful a constitution for the proposed Council of Voluntary Aid, that even the old-established Central Relief Society, which might have been expected to resent this cuckoo in its nest, actually took it under their wing (H. Poole, *The Liverpool Council of Social Service 1909-1959*, Liverpool, Liverpool Council of Social Service, 1960). And lo and behold, modestly installed in an apparently subordinate and totally unthreatening position, his salary raised by voluntary subscribers (amongst them, inevitably, Eleanor Rathbone), there was F. G. D'Aeth, Director of Reports.

Never can there have been a more deceptive job description. D'Aeth had never any doubt that the purpose of writing reports was to provide a basis for action: 'pure' research was a concept not yet dreamed of. In fact, he turned out to be the first of a new breed of social administrator—the prototype back-room boy with a talent for social administration. It is indicative of his attitude to his own role that no one has ever thought of writing his biography; he deliberately diverted attention from himself and refused the offer of an OBE, because publicity would undermine the anonymity which he saw as essential to the job.

> The social work . . . upon which I am engaged is such that quiet unob-trusiveness is a valuable element, and any public recognition of myself might provoke sentiments and undercurrents which would interfere with the progress of our work in general, and the full success of our aims for the social betterment of Liverpool. (Private Letter)

Nothing if not methodical, D'Aeth first tried to get to grips with the chaos revealed by his survey of voluntary effort. Having painstakingly gathered the information about existing charities (he tracked down 65 agencies and 341 churches all engaged in the giving of relief), he tidily grouped them under four heads: the relief of the sick and the afflicted, the relief of those in financial distress, the reformation of character, and, most significantly, the promotion of social improvement. Each group worked through its own sub-committee which acted as a sounding board for opinions and a focus for information, the chair being taken by a prominent business man.

Once marshalled, D'Aeth quickly established a method of directing the energies of his committees. Issues were first raised at the relevant group, often, I suspect, at D'Aeth's instigation. Awareness of some wrong, some of-fence against human dignity, was accompanied by an automatic assumption of the obligation to do something about it. This led to the assembly and ana-lysis of the relevant information and, on that basis, the preparation of a plan of action for its implementation. It was a sequence which is familiar to us nowa-days but was a startling novelty then, especially when applied to charitable work.

D'Aeth's reports were to become a characteristic feature of the CVA in the years that followed: it is from them that the quotations in this chapter are derived. Uniform in size, with covers of a rough grey paper and an art-nou-veau lay-out (which presumably reflect the influence of the artistic Mrs D'Aeth), they represent the working out of a calculated and methodical ap-proach to all manner of problems which previously had been the subject of emotional moralising. Country holidays, Christmas dinners, rescue agencies, were only some of the wide variety of topics each dealt with in turn. His sources of information were equally varied and ingenious; he studied the occupations of the brides and grooms as revealed in church registers, the number of books borrowed from the local library, the number of football teams, the figures of church attendances. He even worked out a tentative minimum standard for play space according to the child population, which, applied to the city as a whole, revealed that 'the inadequacy is glaring'.

A mechanism once established, the first and most pressing of his four tasks was to introduce some sort of order into the particular confusion of relief giving. The ingenuity of 'the poor' in securing assistance and the gullibility of the charitable was topically illustrated by the enterprising mother who managed to secure no less than four Christmas feasts for each of her brood of children. Nobody but D'Aeth would have had the courage to embark on the gargantuan task of persuading both the statutory and the voluntary agencies to support a Mutual Register through which their giving could be coordinated. Apart from the resentment and suspicion which is apt to greet any newcomer to an established field, there was genuine apprehension that the organisation of charitable giving would obliterate the very spontaneous altruism which it was designed to promote. The situation was especially tricky because the co-operation of the three Boards of Guardians was essential to success. Fortunately, the weight of public opinion behind the Royal Commission's report eventually secured their support.

Though the Register was never wholly successful, it served a useful purpose and continued in being until the 1960s when central government's takeover of responsibility for relief ended the need for its existence. However, its real significance, of which D'Aeth was well aware, lay in the fact that it stood for an attempt to explore the possibility of a new relationship between voluntary action and the state. This was a matter for constant concern on the part of the Social Improvement Committee.

If charitable giving was to be methodically organised and 'welfare' increasingly the responsibility of the state as seemed very probable, what scope was left for the individual citizen? That was the question which inescapably haunted the Social Improvement Group. Some of the public rather vaguely assumed that they would now be excused from any further responsibility for the well-being of their fellow men. Many regarded the intrusion of the state, into territory they had previously considered to be their own, as a disaster.

By and large, there was a complete failure to realise that the Report undermined the very foundations of traditional charitable practice. Take, for example, the entirely commendable participation by volunteers in local government services for the health and welfare of children. The provision of free meals for school children had been pioneered by women together with school attendance officers. What more desirable than that this partnership should continue under the auspices of the Education Committee, especially as the demand so far outstripped the capacity of the local authorities to respond? Yet, almost at once, this raised the whole awkward issue of who should pay. Were the charitable in fact assuming a responsibility which should properly be carried by the Education Committee? Or, even more difficult, should the burden of what was surely a health matter, fall on the hospitals which were themselves voluntary bodies? The decorous routine of annual meetings in the Town Hall of the various charities involved became occasions for expressions of bafflement, together with unprecedentedly frank protests against what was regarded as unwarranted intrusion. D'Aeth's skills as a mediator were put to severe test.

With a tiger in its tank of the quality of the Rathbone-Macadam partnership, it is not surprising that it was the Social Improvement Committee that D'Aeth used as the platform from which to confront these issues. The tidying up of the muddle over relief-giving being well in hand, they turned their attention to the promotion of personal service as a corrective to the 'inhumanity' of state provision. As loyal New Testamenteers they were clear that their objective (we would call it their mission today and perhaps the word would, for once, be appropriate) was the betterment of the quality of life of the whole community as distinct from that of the individuals who composed it. All over the country there was talk of town planning, garden cities, and 'the community'; Liverpool was the first of a number of universities that initiated training for town planners. However, by and large, the discussion focused on what we now call the built environment, whereas D'Aeth and his colleagues stuck doggedly to their thesis, that an administrative structure was every bit as essential as a system of drains or street lighting.

Without more ado, D'Aeth set to work to launch a pilot project to prove his point. Beginning with plans for a detailed survey of a neighbourhood, his choice fell on the Netherfield Ward, understandably because that was where the Victoria Settlement was at work. Assistance could be expected from the various groups of voluntary workers based there, such as a local committee of social workers, and from the students and workers in training under the direction of Macadam.

When I first encountered it a decade later, the Netherfield Ward was still pretty much as it must have been in 1912. Many of the people who had worked or lived there were still around. Originally three cottages which had been knocked into one, the Settlement building was one of those comfortable old dwellings which are often to be found in inner areas, marooned in a welter of later, poorer housing. It had been the residence of a local headmaster and cleric, and very pleasant it must have been with its walled garden and a view running down to the river and beyond, all the way to the Welsh hills. 'The lovely retreat of Everton Brow' it had once been called. Not so by the time the Settlement moved in. All the fields between it and the river had been occupied by a great tide of migrant humanity, sucked in by the demand for casual labour for the digging of the docks and the humping of the cargoes. To me as a student, it was enchantingly romantic; rigid lines of close-packed streets of jerry-built houses; gas lamps shining on wet slate roofs; the golden balls of pawnshop; the glittering gaudiness of pubs. All wreathed in the drifting smoke from the innumerable kitchen grates. A Settlement worker once told me that, as a girl, in the garden of her home just across the river, she used to listen to the hum that rose from this dense mass of humanity as it went about its daily affairs. No oil painting this, but a stark black and white etching in the Muirhead Bone style, then so popular, with which we decorated our bed-sit walls.

Conditioned as we are by Coronation Street (or Back Buchananan Street as the local ditty puts it), it is easy to sentimentalise over the destruction of all this and certainly the tower blocks of flats (known as 'the Piggeries') which replaced it, would seem to justify nostalgia for the past. But the picture D'Aeth presented forbids any rosy dreams of the community life of times long past. Granted that many of those who made up the population had brought with them an age-old tradition of the poor helping the poor, and that their translation to an urban setting had reinforced their knowledge of the techniques of survival by mutual defence. Yet, as D'Aeth put it, warm hearts best function within the bony structure of a social structure. This was lacking, 'obliterated in a chaos of streets and houses having no particular beginning or ending'. It was, like the city of which it was a part, a mushroom growth which had only sprung into being in comparatively recent times. This was a transit camp, not an established community; but it was one from which comparatively few ever moved on.

The survey revealed an even more dismaying state of affairs than had been expected. Netherfield was a Ward on paper only. Not a place, just streets without a focus; unidentifiable, with no evident boundaries, certainly not a unity. In a section surely inspired by Booth's great Third Series of inquiries into the *Life and Labour of the People of London* (London, Macmillan, 1883–1903). D'Aeth's team surveyed the social institutions from which strength might be expected to come: 'those organisations that a human being uses in the course of living his or her personal life'. Alas, the churches preached dogmas and doctrines which bred divisive antagonism and hatred, a process that was furthered by the capture of the Orange vote by the Conservatives. Even in my time, shops were barricaded, schools closed, and the Settlement shut its doors on July 12, the day when Orangemen marched the streets. Inevitably, in so conglomerate a community, there was a scarcity of the thrift clubs and friendly societies which redeemed social life in the cotton towns, for example. Trade Unions faced fearsome difficulties in trying to organise themselves in an economy dependent on casual labour and in which there was little scope for women. Political parties merited no mention.

> The residents if left to themselves provide very little: there is only one general attempt in this direction in the Ward. It is that of a social club for men which has a floating attendance of 300.

Opportunities for children's play, or even for people just to get to know their neighbours, simply did not exist. The stimulus which might have come from 'resident educated persons' who worked in the area as teachers or doctors was missing because few lived in the area. In all, Netherfield was a classic instance of what has become typical of inner area life ever since. The consequent low level of aspiration, a major factor in perpetuating acceptance of poor conditions of living, and the curse of the city to this day, provided a formidable obstacle.

Eyeing this dismaying scene, D'Aeth argued that it was futile, as well as bad economy, to focus social reform on assisting individuals whose downfall was due to the lack of opportunities which every normal citizen should have the right to enjoy. The need for the organisation of relief, and the case work associated with it had gained increasing recognition. It was now time for the needs of the community as a whole to be considered and thought given to practical means of strengthening the framework of its social structure. And this, true to the principle of universal social responsibility, D'Aeth firmly declared must be based on local people. Clergy and the like could help, but the responsibility must rest with the residents, because it was their lives that would be affected. With characteristic coolness, he summed up his overall conclusion:

> The subject for responsibility is there, for the town's affairs are urgent and there are many things to be done. Also an inherent sense of responsibility exists in the individual. For lack of bringing the two together, however, the sense of personal responsibility dies.

How was this to be done? It was immediately obvious that some kind of structure, some mechanism for administration was required, for bringing people together for a common purpose. Following on the Poor Law Report, the process of transforming the old Central Relief Society (CRS) committees into Guilds of Help was already in hand with a view to establishing friendly relationships rather than giving material relief, a scheme modelled on the Elberfeld Plan in Germany, which William Rathbone had long advocated. The Victoria Settlement had, in fact, already provided accommodation for precisely such a group. True to form, D'Aeth duly presented a report. The spirit behind the national Guild movement, was, he wrote:

> that of a feeling of fellowship because the problems are in common, of earnestness because the problems are urgent, and of citizenship because the end is the civic good. The purpose of the Guild is to bring together individual inhabitants to promote these activities under the inspiration of this spirit . . . the movement is not a class movement nor is it a movement instigated by prominent individuals. It is essentially a citizen's movement.

To which D'Aeth added a meticulously detailed blue-print of how the Guilds might be organised as vehicles of citizen participation. Membership was to be open to anyone with a general interest in the welfare of the city. The Guilds would be based on the political Wards, with monthly meetings, an annual event in the way of a tea or supper on the first Monday in October, and a united fête in a city park. A Ward handbook would be prepared by each Guild. They would discuss civic problems and indeed, anything of local interest, taking whatever action was necessary. All this strikes us today as being rather over-organised but at the time it stood for a transfer of responsibility from the benefactors to the beneficiaries that was a complete reversal of old style charity based on philanthropic patronage.

It was D'Aeth's dogged pursuit of this 'bringing together' of the citizens and their city, the people and their government, which gives coherence to the remarkably prolific output of the subsequent years. The original Netherfield survey was followed by a long series of inquiries and reports on various aspects of this key theme, which provided the basis for the embryo community development movement (of which, more later). His long track record of support for the attack on what MacCunn called 'the boy problem', took him from the promotion locally of clubs for boys (to match those already available for girls), to the formation of a local federation, and so to the setting up of a national body. Similarly, he built up the Liverpool Council for Voluntary Aid (LCVA) into a powerful 'societies' society' to act as a voice for the voluntary movement and, nationally, was instrumental in founding the National

Council for Voluntary Service (NCVS). In addition, he contributed to the journals and conferences of the developing social sciences.

I was told by social workers who had worked with him that his obsession with co-ordination sometimes exasperated free-thinking Liverpudlians, but they never questioned the vision that lay behind it. His target was the social malaise that afflicted society as a whole; not the relief of the ill-fare of individuals, but the advancement of the well-fare of the community to which they belonged. In that context, he saw the voluntary movement as a complementary service to that of the state, a bulwark against the deprivation of personal responsibility. The aim must be an equal partnership. The going would be long and hard. But before they could get to grips with this situation the outbreak of the war in 1914 brought changes to the scene such as neither he nor the Social Improvement Group could ever have foreseen.

We were in Scotland when war was declared. My father's family had once been farmers in Perthshire before they migrated to Glasgow, so every summer we rented some small habitation in a remote glen or barren moor and with a cargo of linen, cutlery, fishing gear and model boats, loyally returned to our native heath. That particular year, 1914, we were at the Post Office in Strath Tummel, the postman and his family obligingly sleeping under the counter in the corrugated iron shed that served as shop. When news trickled through of the outbreak of hostilities, filled with apprehension, we upped stakes and headed for home which was London at that stage. It was a long day's journey because we were continually shunted into sidings to let trains full of waving troops go by.

Though I didn't know it at the time, of course, the entire scope and scale of women's lives—of my own life—were about to be altered beyond comprehension. No-one could ever say of the First World War what became the flip comment of the Second, that they had 'had a good war'. No good ever came of that particular holocaust. But rapid and irreversible change it certainly brought about, for women more than anyone else.

Four years later, still in London, I was walking home from school across Ealing Green when the sirens sounded and I knew that the war was over. Even at the age of twelve, I had sensibility enough to be awed by the feeling of occasion. Innocent that I was, slouching along in my gymslip and school hat, I had no idea of what lay ahead for me and my generation or of what was even at that moment taking place in the Liverpool to which I was shortly to be transferred as a consequence of a family move.

Chapter 4
BIRTH OF THE
SOCIAL WORKER

In which the pressure of mass deprivation brought about by the First War necessitated the acceptance of state intervention and the raising of standards of service. The consequent gradual exclusion of voluntary workers intensified the dilemma of how to combine the right of the individual to social responsibility with the practice of a statutory system of welfare.

When the war started in 1914, no one was prepared for the wholesale distress caused by the call-up of so many of the bread-winners on whom entire families depended. The poor had always been with them but the avalanche of need that now swamped the existing relief agencies revealed the existence of a new kind of poor; people whose poverty was nothing to do with whether they were deserving or otherwise, and whose numbers were on a scale far beyond anything previously experienced. Desperate families searched here, there, everywhere for even the barest means of subsistence—the demands for assistance far exceeded the available resources.

Accustomed as we now are to the bureaucratic state, the lack of the mere mechanics of assistance is hard to imagine. The only appropriate organisation already in being in Liverpool was the Soldiers' and Sailors' Families Association (SSAFA), set up during the Boer War to meet the needs of servicemen's dependants. This had dwindled to a mere thirteen members, with no subscription list. In this crisis, it was to Eleanor Rathbone that the Lord Mayor understandably turned; she was by now a person of considerable standing, a City Councillor, with long experience as a District Visitor, and in a position to rally voluntary workers through her association with the Victoria Settlement.

Elizabeth Macadam was later to recollect that:

> the resurrection of this moribund body at lightning speed was one of the triumphs in the history of voluntary effort. (Elizabeth Macadam, *The New Philanthropy*, London, Allen & Unwin, 1934, p. 56)

Within weeks the work was organised, the city mapped out into twenty-nine districts, and some 10,000 cases a week were being dealt with. To Eleanor, as to so many of the women who rallied round her, the experience brought deep satisfaction in that, at last, they were able to play a part in the city's affairs in a way which stretched their capabilities to limits never thought possible. An Oxford friend who encountered her in the post-war period was astonished to find that:

> the absent minded philosopher of College days had become the admirably efficient organiser she proved herself to be. (Stocks, op. cit., p. 75)

Nevertheless, satisfying though the organisation of SSAFA might be, its scope was necessarily limited. Beyond it, chaos reigned, triggered off by the emotional reaction of the public to the unaccustomed experience of total warfare. Elizabeth Macadam remarked that:

> The nervous energy of those who had to stay at home when others went to the front seemed to find an outlet in starting brand new societies; ancient and forgotten charitable agencies woke from their slumbers in a burst of patriotism. (Macadam, op. cit., p. 56)

Inevitably, in view of the reputation for coordination that he had already won, D'Aeth was seconded to the Town Hall to tackle the task of introducing some degree of coherence into this plethora of activity. Working closely with Eleanor and the Victoria Settlement, this he succeeded in doing, but Liverpool was one of the few exceptions to the general state of confusion. Elsewhere things came to such a pass that it was necessary to intervene by legislation, and, in 1917, after a deal of argument and tinkering, the entire responsibility for the administration of pensions was handed over to a specially created Ministry.

The fact that when, eventually, a local War Pensions Committee was set up in Liverpool, it agreed to work through the existing voluntary agencies was a plume in Eleanor's cap but she and her colleagues were well aware of the significance of what was happening. The inevitability of state intervention might have to be accepted—indeed, was to be welcomed—but what scope then would there be for the exercise of social responsibility by the individual in that brave new world?

> All those who believe in freely given public service as distinct from and as a necessary supplement to State Compulsion, must stand together, in order to give effect to their work

D'Aeth asserted. But how was this to be done?

In the light of what we now know was yet to come, it is hard for us today to understand the mood of idealism which marked the early years of the war. The realisation that in future the state must inevitably take over responsibility for the great bulk of the relief of poverty, which had previously been left to individual conscience, seemed to set people free to plan and to dream. As early as 1915, D'Aeth actually prepared a report on the *Future of Personal Service* which was a blueprint for ensuring that the spirit of wartime service would be carried on into the peace. Nothing came of that attempt but, two years later, in 1917, the wishful thought that the war must surely end soon persuaded the LCVA that the moment had come for action.

A Town Hall meeting, with as much of the usual panache as circumstances permitted, was duly organised at which Elizabeth Macadam addressed the company on 'The Future of the Voluntary Worker', pointing out the importance of voluntary action and the necessity of ensuring its continuation after the war, 'though possibly in a somewhat wider form'. [CVA. July 1917.] Public reaction was reasonably favourable, but the war did not, in fact, end and, for the moment, the impetus was lost. Nevertheless, drained though they were by the years of war work, and so driven that the only time they could meet was late on a Saturday morning, a tiny handful of the faithful gathered in Eleanor's office to plan the next move. Only six were present, but what a six, including as it did D'Aeth, Macadam and the young Warden of the Men's Settlement, Fred Marquis (later Lord Woolton). It is clear from the records that they knew exactly what they were after; all that had to be determined was how it was to be brought about.

The aim was to organise voluntary work in such a way that it would complement and not supplant the services of the state. It was vitally important that the universal right to state benefits should be matched by ensuring the right of every citizen to give practical expression to their sense of social concern by personal service. The plan was to set up an agency that would be a focus for 'a permanent comprehensive body of voluntary social workers for friendly visiting and other purposes'. This was to be a development of what was already in existence in the shape of Guilds of Help. There would be a central office and divisional sub-offices, each adequately staffed. Committees on a Ward or District basis would be grouped round these offices and much care was to be taken to ensure that the people involved were genuinely representative of the neighbourhood.

There were, of course, endless difficulties. Other voluntary agencies reacted with defensive zeal against anything that looked like encroachment on their territory. The general public were not convinced of the need for friendly visiting. The bogey of finance inevitably rattled its chains. Most importantly, the lesson of experience was that a trained leader would be essential (a voluntary worker of the calibre of Eleanor could not be guaranteed). By a combination of influence in the right places, adroit negotiation, and luck, the difficulties were overcome. On 18 July 1918, just as the war was about to end, Dorothy Keeling arrived to take up responsibility for the Liverpool Association for Personal Service (hereafter PSS; the name was only adopted in 1922, but I use it for convenience throughout).

Aged thirty-eight when she came to Liverpool, Dorothy Keeling was of the same generation as Eleanor Rathbone. The daughter of the Headmaster of Bradford Grammar School, she had acquired considerable experience of voluntary charitable agencies whilst in London, including acting as Secretary of the National Association of Guilds of Help, for which she was awarded an OBE. She was never clear as to the origins of her interest in social work as a career in preference to teaching (the usual outlet for young women in search of occupation). Possibly it was because she suffered from a rather distressing breathing difficulty, like a stammer in reverse, which would surely have been a handicap in a classroom. She herself spoke of an unresolved feeling of guilt provoked by her encounters with sick and bedridden old men when visiting the Bradford Workhouse, but I suspect that beneath this lay the driving force of what Josephine Butler once described as the awesome burden of compassion.

Whatever the truth, Dorothy Keeling was a driven woman, always at the mercy of an acute sensibility to injustice; over-ambitious to achieve the righting of wrongs, cruelly zealous in her demands on herself and those who worked for her. Her life was punctuated by breakdowns when she reached and passed the point of utter exhaustion. Sir John Hobhouse, once her chairman, remarked:

> If I have been unduly severe with you at times, it has not been for want of admiration of your remarkable qualities, but because dynamic people require someone to sit on their heads occasionally to prevent too much damage to the surrounding scenery. (Dorothy Keeling, *The Crowded Stairs*, London, National Council of Social Service, 1961, p. 130)

Small in stature, with a sharp nose, and an even sharper tongue, her insistence on hard thought and high principles, her implacable standards of efficiency and the acidity with which she expressed her forthright opinions, made her an awkward person to know. The reality was even more forbidding than the myth. As students, we shrank back from the prospect of doing 'practicals' under her super-vision, and her high-handed treatment of committee and staff alike was the stuff of local legend. Her passionate egalitarianism sat oddly alongside her loyalty to the traditions of the class from which she came. (She once stayed the night with me and noting that I served her breakfast in bed on a bare tray—as was then the fashion—her subsequent letter of thanks was duly accompanied by a white crochet traycloth!).

Dorothy Keeling's first move was to survey the city by tram, sitting on the open front seat upstairs with a map spread on her knees, learning the lie of the land and getting the feel of the wards and districts into which her vast territory was divided. The gulf between haves and have-nots, which it was her mission to surmount, was immediately and painfully evident. In her autobiography she wrote:

> Liverpool, when I came to it, was a city notable for its striking contrasts; its great wealth and devastating poverty; its comfortable and even luxurious homes and its appalling slums; its derelict schools and steadily rising majestic cathedral. It was the only place in England which had, and, so far as I know, ever had, its two kinds of tram cars: first class, with white exteriors and blue velvet seats, in which there always seemed to be plenty of room, and in which double fares were charged downstairs, and dirty grimy and usually overcrowded second class. These first class cars were introduced in 1908 and were finally discontinued in 1923. (Keeling, op. cit.)

Had the PSS been able to test the situation by some kind of pilot project, as was D'Aeth's usual practice, a more cautious start might have been made. As it was, Dorothy Keeling inherited the overblown situation created by the war; based on the work of Eleanor Rathbone, there were already in existence no less than 16 local committees, serving 21 out of the city's 37 wards. Right from the start it was apparent that there was a far greater volume of work than anyone had bargained for. The existing case load of the two Settlements alone, when Dorothy took over, was 1459, and demobilisation following the end of the war inevitably brought a massive demand for help and advice.

The committee had anticipated that it would never escape from the dilemma of how to combine the offer of friendly help with a refusal to give material relief. What it had failed to foresee, not surprisingly because it was something never before experienced, was the paradox that the more generous the provision made by the statutory services, the greater would be the demand for precisely the sort of advice and support the PSS was designed to offer.

Hundreds of our poorer citizens have obtained, through the guidance of the Personal Service Committee, just the material, medical or friendly help which they needed but which they did not know how to obtain. Sometimes it is a difficult form to be filled up, sometimes a recommendation to be obtained. Sometimes there is sheer ignorance of the advantages to which, as citizens, they are entitled, and of the resources at their disposal. The very multiplicity of the societies and agencies merely increases their bewilderment. (PSS, *Annual Report*, Liverpool, 1922)

Imperceptibly, by sheer weight of numbers, the emphasis shifted from the original purpose of promoting friendly contacts between individuals to that of ensuring that all those in need were enabled to enjoy whatever benefits the State provided. So much so that, in the *Annual Report* for 1922 (from which the following quotations are taken), the aims of the Society were redefined to give pride of place to

securing for Liverpool citizens the full benefits of social legislation and other administrative measures (public and voluntary) for their welfare, and for this purpose ... to unite voluntary workers who undertake enquiries and friendly visiting.

Amidst the volume of work which now pours into Byrom Hall lent to them free by the City Mission continuously all the year round it is sometimes difficult not to lose sight of the first object for which the Society was founded, viz., the friendly visiting of those in trouble or difficulty who need the support and guidance of a friend. The idea is to give to each visitor a very limited number of cases at a time, but the practice is at present very far from the ideal. That can only be achieved if the supply of workers keeps pace with the volume of the work.

Dorothy's target was to have a hundred district committees with ten voluntary workers on each. She asserted confidently that:

in a city of three quarters of a million people, it should not be difficult to find a thousand men and women willing to undertake to visit two or three families and to attend a monthly committee meeting.

Alas, the supply of volunteers never did keep up with the torrent of work which descended on the Society. For all her brave talk, the harsh reality was that, even with the boost given by lingering wartime enthusiasm:

nearly all the local Committees are understaffed, and many of the Wards in the most densely populated areas already need several committees if the work is to be thoroughly and effectively done.

The consequences were disturbing.

At present, far too much of the work is done by officials, the Secretaries of the District Offices—this is by no means the object of the Committee ... the large majority of the cases need far more than can be given by the Office Secretaries with their constant and ever in-creasing stream of new cases needing immediate treatment. We should like, after the first visit has been paid, to hand over 75% of the cases to voluntary workers, who through sympathy, friendship and encouragement, can restore self-dependence and self-respect, can give hope to the downcast, and cheer to the sick and lonely—can, in short, be friends to the people entrusted to their care.

Nor was this all. Behind the chronic shortage of voluntary workers, and the magnitude of the demands made upon the Society, there lay concealed another factor which was to have consequences such as to threaten the very purpose of the society. This was the simple fact that the problems of the post-war world called for an expertise and a competence which were far beyond, and quite different from, that normally to be expected from even the friendliest of friendly visitors. As early as 1921, Dorothy had noted in her annual report that:

Without a wide knowledge of conditions and how to improve them, the social workers may do more harm than good. It is, therefore, essential in a Society whose main work is done by voluntary workers, most of whom have a very limited amount of time to spare, to have a permanent, trained and experienced staff to guide and direct them. During the last month of the year the office was crowded every day with people who wanted detailed and technical information of all kinds. A staff of four all told is very inadequate to supervise the work of 5,500 cases, to train students, to direct over 100 voluntary workers, to organise committees of various sorts, to keep office records, to conduct a large correspondence, to interview callers of many varieties, etc.

The outcome was inevitably that the PSS had to employ more paid staff and that they must have been trained for the job. That apart, Dorothy Keeling's insistence on standards of immaculate efficiency was enough in itself to ensure that the part-time volunteer would be reduced to a status inferior to that of the professional worker. Tribute was paid in the Annual Reports to the valiant contribution of the volunteers but it was increasingly in their capacity as handmaids. Anecdotes about how Dorothy treated even the daughters of the wealthiest patrons of the Society bear testimony to the acceptance by both sides of the lowly status of the volunteer.

To its credit, the PSS was one of the first voluntary societies to employ a full-time training officer but the training of volunteers was always spasmodic; they were regarded as amateur professionals rather than professional amateurs, and the gulf between friendly visitor and professional worker inevitably widened. It was only late in life that Dorothy reflected that the emphasis on the qualified worker might best have been offset by the provision of a different and more appropriate training for the voluntary workers.

All these pressures notwithstanding, Dorothy clung doggedly to her conviction that voluntary personal service was the universal principle upon which a human society must operate. The work of a Friendly Visitor, she insisted, was

> ... essentially work for amateurs, in the truest and most literal meaning of the word—men and women who give their personal service for love—love of God, love of their City, love of the community and love of the individual family, for it is this spirit which forms the whole basis of the Personal Service Committee.

Yet, though her loyalty to the aims of the PSS was never shaken, the logic of events forced her to develop a second and complementary vision as to where the future lay. It was a vision of the Urban Society as one in which freedom from deprivation was regarded as a right of citizenship and not a charitable benefaction. As such, it must necessarily be a state responsibility; only collective action could possibly meet need on such a scale as daily confronted her. It was equally clear to her that the right of the individual to benefit from membership of a society must carry with it an automatic duty to give to the community as well as receive from it. The denial of the opportunity to fulfil this obligation suffered by far too many of the people, was an injustice that called for nothing less than changes in the system of governance. At what point she joined the Communist Party as a means to this end was her own business, but it was certainly an expression of her commitment to the creation of a 'communitarian' society.

I don't think she ever contemplated becoming a City Councillor herself, but, under her leadership, the PSS became an important element in the political scene, to all intents and purposes, the champion of the individual against the encroaching tide of state control. It was not enough to guide applicants through the tangle of bureaucratic rules and regulations, so as to ensure that they enjoyed that which was theirs by virtue of their citizen-ship; the Society must also utilise its first-hand know-ledge of the condition of the people as ammunition in the fight to safeguard their rights and their dignity. We watched with glee and deep respect as Dorothy Keeling took on the various giants who threatened her path. The Public Assistance Committee (the Department of Social Security [DSS] of the day), pawnbrokers and money lenders, hire purchase firms and betting offices, who tempted people to spend money they could not afford, were all the targets of highly effective campaigns.

What she preached, she practised. Convinced by experience that gambling was a cause of widespread misery, no money was ever raised by the PSS other than by direct giving apart from the annual sale of work and occasional entertainments at which no raffles or tombolas were permitted. When the 17th Earl of Derby threatened to withdraw his Patronage of the Society on hearing of her anti-gambling campaign (he being a confirmed racegoer), she secured the unanimous support of her Committee for her stand. Lord Derby duly resigned.

Not everyone shared Dorothy Keeling's vision, or her realism. The story of the long struggle by those loyal to the charitable tradition of the past to cling to their principles in face of the expansion of State responsibility, makes sad reading. It is obvious to us today that they had no option but to face the fact of the emerging Welfare State, but the implications of this were hard to accept and painful to endure.

The prime example of this was, inevitably in that day and age, a woman, a spinster, and a voluntary worker. How Margaret Beavan attempted to come to terms with the on-coming tide of universal state provision is a tale of suicidal heroism. She was a Queen Canute who refused to relinquish her stand even when the waters of the incoming tide washed right over her head. Factually speaking, her story is an easy one to tell. Born in 1877 she was of the same vintage as Eleanor Rathbone and Dorothy Keeling. She attended the Belvedere School, not so much because of any great zeal on the part of her family for the emancipation of women as because its moral tone supported that of the Sefton Park Presbyterian Church where they came under the influence of Dr John Watson, a leading local preacher.

On leaving school there was, of course, no suggestion that she should earn her own living, though she did go to the Royal Holloway College to train as a teacher. Her specific interest in child welfare arose out of a meeting of the Old Girls' Association at Belvedere when she responded to an appeal by a speaker from the Victoria Settlement for help with a class for crippled children who were unable to attend ordinary schools. Her subsequent championship of the cause of child welfare could not have been more apt to the climate of the times when recognition of the needs of children was gaining ground. Taken together with her implacable determination to 'do something' with her life, work rapidly expanded in all manner of directions. What followed provides a quite exceptional example of individual achievement based on little else other than:

> the most stubborn exercise of will power which would have been condemned as wilfulness had it not been channelled into so splendid and deserving an object. (Ivy Ireland, *Margaret Beavan of Liverpool*, Liverpool, Henry Young, 1938)

Under the umbrella of the Invalid Children's Association (ICA), the agency devised as a platform for her activities, she pioneered a remarkable range of services for child care. The climax to this life of total commitment came with the opening of Leasowe Bank in 1913. This was an Open Air Hospital, with beds for no less than two hundred children with TB, set in a fine open site of nearly fourteen acres, adjacent to the Wallasey Embankment on the south side of Liverpool Bay. Four special trains brought VIPs galore to the ceremony to applaud this astonishing achievement by a voluntary society.

Like Dorothy Keeling, Margaret Beavan's track record was therefore such as to enable her to command considerable respect in the search for reconstruction when peace was declared. Her response could not have been more different. She lacked the intellectual capacity to analyse the situation or the political principle on which to build a strategy for dealing with it. She accepted what she regarded as the take-over of voluntary action by the state because there was no practical alternative—indeed, she milked them of official resources quite brilliantly—but she never resolved the question of the respective rôles and responsibilities of statutory and voluntary action.

The Authorities, the Medical Officer of Health and the Education Committee in particular, were glad enough to enlist the service of the ICA in work for which they were being forced to accept a responsibility, but for which they had themselves neither the money nor even the inclination.

Addressing the Maternity and Child Welfare Conference in London in 1922 it was painfully clear that Margaret Beavan was at a loss in the strange circumstances of the post-war era. With increasing desperation, she protested her conviction that the day of the voluntary worker was far from done but she was unable to define what that rôle should now be.

The chronic drain on the resources and the workers of the ICA impelled her to extremes of publicity so that at times the woes of the children seemed almost to become fodder for money-raising campaigns rather than the reverse. The mothers, she once remarked, were invaluable for propaganda work. The intensity of her commitment and the ferocity with which she drove herself (and all those with whom she came into contact), provoked a sense of near awe, even half a century later.

Nevertheless, she was an anachronism in the shifting scene of the 1920s. An invitation to stand as a City Councillor seemed to offer an escape from her predicament. She needed new fields to conquer; but, that apart, she was a conservative by character rather than conviction and had no political programme to offer. Her election would be a recognition of services rendered, not a promise for the future. Against the advice of her friends, she stood for, and won, the Princes Park ward (by coincidence, to become part of the ward I was myself to represent years later). As a Councillor, she skilfully played statutory agencies against voluntary, using the one to eke out the resources of the other. To celebrate her twenty-five years of service as a voluntary worker, she was given a Civic Banquet in 1926, and a year later, was awarded the remarkable distinction of becoming the first woman Lord Mayor of Liverpool. Greatly relishing her rôle as little-local-girl-made-good, she flooded the Town Hall with guests who had never set foot in it before.

Her subsequent political career was a disaster. The Conservatives, unscrupulously one cannot help but think, cashed in on her popularity by asking her to fight the Everton election for them in 1929. The anticipated triumph of sentiment for the 'little mother' never materialised: instead she was caught up in one of the most brutal of Liverpool's long tradition of savage elections. In its place, the rising tide of resentment against patronage and philanthropy, the simmering bulk of criticism against the ICA because it was designed to maintain the *status quo* and not reform it, suddenly confronted her. Asked what she had to say about the spectre of unemployment which haunted the future, she could only point to her past endeavours. She was called Maggie Mussolini because of the cordiality of her visit to Italy as Lord Mayor. When the issue of public grant aid for Catholic schools broke surface, the whole campaign went up in a sheet of flame. A mini-Ulster situation developed in which she was physically buffeted. The descriptions of the meetings she gallantly attended, right to the end of this bitter campaign, and of the treatment she encountered in the very alleys and courts where she had once been greeted with adulation and affection, make one weep for her. Those who saw her during the Everton election were irresistibly reminded of the aristocrats during the French Revolution.

The rocket of her meteoric career was fast falling. She retreated to her old base, the ICA, but never regained her popularity in the city. There was an air of hostility which baffled her workers. The costs of running what was, virtually, a city-wide universal child care service were piling up into debts of menacing proportions. Her only answer was to set herself to organise yet another Great Fair in St George's Hall in 1930. By superhuman effort, the total raised was an unbelievable £30,000; unbelievable because unemployment was already hanging heavy over the city. It was immediately followed by an equally spectacular Children's Party, again in St George's Hall, at which 1000 sat down to 'food and fun', whilst parents and well-wishers crowded the galleries to observe the proceedings. Exhausted, she died a few weeks later, aged 54.

I never had much personal contact with 'Maggie' because we social science students so strongly disapproved of her ways of working, but my recollection of the fury her goings-on aroused in my generation is surprisingly vivid. No doubt we were jealous that this dainty little mouse of a human being should have achieved so much. Her flair for showmanship, her exposure of the children as material for fundraising, her personal success in the remorseless pursuit of her own way of doing things, all these irritated me and my kind. I fear we were intellectual prigs with our high principles and spartan living. I don't think that I ever took part in the Annual Rag Week to raise funds for charity— though a bit of student fun would have done me good. Nevertheless, our reaction was evidence of a deep difference of stance. Our hope for the future lay in an entirely new approach to the problem of poverty.

It was a painful irony that the consequence of what amounted to the professionalising of charitable work in the post-war years should have been the virtual denial to others of that very right to be of service that had inspired the women's bid for emancipation. This is not in any way to denigrate the achievements of that generation of Amazon women. The times required an organised and skilled approach to the relief of distress. It was not only inevitable but necessary that this should find expression in the development of professionalism. But it cannot be denied that the input of the tide of women hungry for opportunity after the war pushed the development of the social services right off what might have been expected in the normal course of events, and in the process, slowly but surely suffocated the right to 'love their neighbour' of the individual.

Dorothy Keeling was surely right when she shifted her target from the promotion of personal service to the much wider aim of creating a society in which the practice of social responsibility would be viable. A century or more ago, her predecessors had concluded that the spiritual civilisation of the poor must be complemented by the civilising of the material environment. The Urban Ideal had pushed the boundaries forward by demanding the civilising of society itself: in the post-war world charity must be once more redefined. It was with extreme reluctance that Dorothy abandoned her commitment to this task when the outbreak of the Second War presented her with the opportunity to set up an advice service on a national scale. To the end, she clung to the hope that the Citizens' Advice Bureaux would incorporate people of all classes, voluntarily giving of their time, in the spirit of the true Friendly Visitor.

Meanwhile, D'Aeth with quite remarkable consistency of purpose and despite the stresses and disruptions of war-time, had never ceased to beaver away at the creation of that strong social structure which he believed to be essential if the principle of individual social responsibility was to be viable. His genius lay in his talent for spotting the relevance of any enterprise, however trivial, to that overall purpose and the exigencies of war had given him exceptional scope for its exercise. Liverpool, like many other large cities, had, he advised the LCVA in discussing plans for post-war reconstruction, failed to make use of the potential for service of the bulk of its population. This he attributed to the lack of adequate machinery of organisation; this was 'an important subject to which so far public attention has not been given'. War or no war, it was to remedy this defect that he had been unshakeably committed.

His freedom for action was facilitated when in 1917, the LCVA at last extricated itself from its association with the CRS which continued to reiterate its dedication to the giving of material relief. Freed from this tie, the LCVA moved into its own office at 14, Castle Street from which it operates to this day. Master in his own house, D'Aeth proceeded to expand its activities from the original discreet intention to introduce method into the muddle of existing charitable effort into a programme for the active promotion of a wide variety of projects. Under the banner of the newly reconstituted Social Improvement Group, and after infinitely careful preparatory work in the way of reports and surveys, he gathered about him groups of people, each dedicated to the promotion of some particular interest. Unmarried mothers, the bastardy laws, cheap tram fares for children on holiday, health education, whatever emerged as an issue of concern was found a place under the umbrella of the LCVA. Margaret Beavan chaired an impressive gathering of public health workers as a vehicle for education and reform. The office in Castle Street became a launching pad for a proliferation of inter-locking projects, all designed to provide opportunities for the exercise of social responsibility. In one corner, space was found for the newly-appointed organiser for the Citizens' Institutes, in another for the Secretary of the Liverpool Union of Girls' Clubs and embryo Juvenile Organisations' Committee. The setting up of a Union of Boys' Clubs constituted yet another cog in the machinery to which the bringing into existence of the PSS was yet another contribution. D'Aeth's appetite for system building extended far beyond the purely local and he was instrumental in the creation of the national network for the coordination of youth and community work with which we are familiar today.

The members of the original Social Improvement Group on whom he had been accustomed to rely, had each gone their separate ways. Macadam, having made a name for herself during the war as the pioneer of the new specialism of personnel workers, decided to devote herself to the training of social workers in general and moved to London. Eleanor Rathbone looked increasingly to politics for the opportunity to promote her ideas; she stood for Toxteth in 1922 and the Combined Universities, which she won in 1929.

Much more challenging was the attitude adopted by the young man referred to by us as Freddie Marquis, Warden of the Men's University Settlement and a lively contributor to the Social Improvement Group. A science graduate, his reaction to what he saw in the streets round the Settlement was one of neither pity nor guilt but of sheer disbelief and disgust. In words that exactly echo those of D'Aeth in describing his own early days as a curate, he wrote:

> For the most part the problem of poverty is not the problem of the able-bodied willing person, unable to sell his labour; it is the problem of the whole mass of physically, mentally, and morally diseased people, perpetually inefficient, blind to their own welfare, ignorant of the prospects of their offspring, and rendered content in their condition by mutual association. (King, *The Two Nations*, op. cit.)

Angered by what he regarded as the failure of the working man to secure 'a life for his soul and a life for his children's bodies', Marquis became increasingly sure that the only hope for the future lay in the emergence of an elite 'controlling class' which would exercise authority on the basis of consent freely given by an educated work-force. (It is a philosophy that I was astonished to encounter years later in the person of Michael Heseltine when he visited Liverpool in his capacity as Minister for Merseyside in the 1980s.) Loyal to his convictions, he moved on to become a Managing Director of Lewis's, a large department store. We watched fascinated as the zeal for reform of the young socialist with his red tie was translated into the positively feudal paternalism of Lord Woolton, Minister of Food under a Tory government in the Second War.

It comes as no surprise that in the context of such a rapidly developing climate of opinion D'Aeth should have turned his attention to the need for trained workers and to the provision of courses to meet it. Together with the growing interest in a more scientific approach to social reform, this added up to an unanswerable case and I cannot help but suppose that it was at D'Aeth's instigation that a practical proposal was put forward. What finally emerged was a proposal to build on the foundations which he himself, and Macadam as his successor had laid at the School of Social Science at the University.

Chapter 5
THE STUDY OF SOCIETY

In which as the first student to take a degree in social science, I am introduced to the study of society at Liverpool University. I describe the slow growth of community development in terms of my own experience of unemployment centres, community councils, and youth work, and consider the consequences for the voluntary movement of the emancipation of women.

The decision as to what form a memorial to Charles Booth should take had been deferred because he died during the war. However, in 1922 it was eventually decided to press ahead with the endowment of a Charles Booth Chair of Social Science at the University of Liverpool. It was an admirably appropriate decision because Booth had not only been a Liverpool shipowner but had pioneered the study of society with his great survey of the *Life and Labour of the People of London* (op. cit., p. 69). The spirit of reconstruction was in the air. The war stood for a clean sweep of old ideas and old ways of doing things. The spontaneous philanthropy of the past must give way to a planned and organised attack on the problem of poverty. What more appropriate memorial to the great pioneer of the application of scientific method to social conditions could there be than a tangible commitment to the furtherance of the approach he had pioneered. The School of Social Science, as the new Professor declared in his Inaugural Lecture, was to be a centre of citizenship as well as of teaching and research.

The announcement was greeted with laudatory cries of approbation; another Liverpool first, it was proudly claimed. There was, of course, no precedent as to what species of academic should be invited to fill the post. How the choice was made, I don't know, but Alexander Carr Saunders was certainly an extraordinarily sophisticated character to walk on to the Liverpool stage. Educated at Eton and Oxford, detached of mind and with a consuming interest in biology and eugenics, he made no attempt to conceal the wry astonishment with which he eyed his new circumstances.

As a biologist he must have seemed an unlikely candidate but the post was a novelty and no job specification had yet been drawn up. As things turned out, he was years ahead of his time in stressing the importance of the group rather than the individual as the unit of survival, whether in the animal kingdom or the human. He must have been one of the few people at that period to grasp the implications of the destruction of communities which the slum clearance programme involved. He was certainly one of the first to call attention to the importance of what we now call defensible space:

> the territory occupied by each group and the conventions and rituals as well as the fighting by which that territory was denied to outsiders. (H. P. Brown, 'Memoir of A. M. Carr Saunders', *Proceedings of the British Academy*, 1967)

Hence the study of society rather than the training of social workers to do individual casework was his concept of the function of a department of social science. Hence, too, his plans for the initiation in 1931 of the Merseyside Survey on the basis of a Rockefeller grant, something Charles Booth had hoped to do but never achieved. This was intended to be both a record of the city at a particular point in time and a basis for action. 'The immediate aim is to ascertain social conditions, the ultimate aim is to improve them', wrote Caradog Jones, the meticulous Welshman who struggled to teach us statistics (Caradog Jones, *Social Survey of Merseyside*, Liverpool, Liverpool University Press, 1934). Whether Carr Saunders was equally optimistic, I rather doubt. To an inquiry as to whether Liverpool would provide him with profitable academic material, he replied that it was as rewarding to study a society in decay as in its heyday.

I had at that stage no interest in social problems. I had gone to the 'slums' for the simple reason that it was in girls' clubs that country dancing flourished most happily; I had been a folk song and dance addict ever since I had met Cecil Sharp, the folk-music collector, while at school. I was never attracted by the esoterics of casework and shrank from first-hand contact with the realities of poverty for which public school life had not prepared me. I found it acutely embarrassing to meet 'the poor', dressed in a handsome black coat lavishly trimmed with fox fur which my kind mother had bought me in an effort to make me more attractive, but it never occurred to me to seek to do good to the girls I met in the clubs. I was, on the contrary, preoccupied with my own need to understand the world in which I found myself, what made the great city tick, and what was my own relationship with it and its people. No wonder my heart leapt when I heard of the appointment of a Professor of Social Science at the University of Liverpool and of his intention to promote the study of society.

At first, I was his only degree student, a singularly immature public school product, dumb as a cluck, trained to absorb information without argument. The other students who were taking the existing certificate course were all much older, a group of fifteen or twenty assorted middle-class, middle-aged women, some clergy and the like, plus a couple of working-class men who had come up through the Workers' Educational Association (WEA). The certificate was essentially a qualification for case work and some of the students hoped to take posts in a voluntary agency. The School was then housed in Bedford Street in a nice little stucco villa, though barred and bolted like a prison because it had previously been used as an armoury by the Officers' Training Corps. Later, we moved to larger premises on the corner of Abercromby Square and eventually into the considerable grandeur of what had been the Bishop's Palace, a few doors further along, officially 'opened' by William Beveridge in 1931. 'Prof' electrified us by hanging Medici prints of naked ladies emerging from seashells on the bare walls of our lecture rooms. The gesture was symptomatic of a personal concern and commitment to betterment, ours and the city's, such as had characterised the University in the days of the 'New Testament'.

> He entered readily into the personal relations of a civic university, dining with the merchant princes of the University Council, gathering students in his flat, walking with them in the Welsh hills. (H. P. Brown, op. cit.)

Sadly, I appreciate all this with after-thought only. As his solitary degree student, what an opportunity I was presented with: yet when I left the University in 1928, duly capped and gowned as the first-ever student to take an Honours Degree in Social Science, all I had in the hand was a shamingly poor second. My heart had never been in academic study, my mind never provoked from sleep. It can only have been because public relations required that the first candidate in a brand new course should succeed that I was awarded even that lowly result.

Nevertheless, I had enjoyed life enormously. I had been a regular helper at the Eleanor Rathbone Holiday School at the Victoria Settlement, where the children were so hungry that they ate the raw macaroni 'beads' provided for a handicraft class. I had toured every Women's Institute in Lancashire with my repertoire of twelve folk instruments, from penny whistle to accordion, earning my pocket money in the process. I had taught country dancing in various youth clubs round the city, where rests between dances were essential if the undernourished unemployed members were to last out the whole evening. It had never occurred to me or to anyone else that all the fun I had was in fact a practical exploration of what Carr Saunders was trying to teach us about the importance of groups as the stuff of the study of society. Somehow the connection was never made, or if it was, it was deplored as a distraction from scientific study such as sociology was then aspiring to be.

Thus ill-equipped, I stepped out into the chill reality of a world which could hardly have been less welcoming. I was not wanted. There was no room for the likes of me. Ahead of me and my generation was that whole regiment of women who had escaped from domesticity into wartime activity but now were left stranded by the end of the hostilities. Competent, dedicated and willing to work for a pittance as they were, what hope had we youngsters against their experience and maturity. All I myself could offer was a shabby degree in a subject few people recognised, designed to equip me for a career in the administration of the public services or some such deskbound occupation. My poor achievement ruled that out. In those dark days of economic catastrophe, I knew that I would be lucky if I found a job of any kind, let alone one that was congenial or adequately paid. (Ah me, those endless student debates on the morality of charitable organisations that ran on the sweated labour of single women.) Moreover, to the common experience of unemployment was added the crushing load of the need for us as women to justify competing against men with families to keep.

My involvement in folk-dancing in girls' clubs led to my being offered a temporary job as organiser of a huge Pageant of Youth through the streets of Liverpool, the sort of carnival at which Liverpudlians excel. This was designed to boost support for the club movement by presenting young people in a more attractive light than was customary. I enjoyed myself enormously and determined that being a youth worker was the life for me, in spite of the ill-concealed disappointment of those who had trained me that I should opt for what they regarded as a lowly occupation.

Unfortunately for me, few if any of the girls' clubs or adult centres could afford paid workers and the embryo community movement out on the new estates (of which more later), had to fight to gain recognition of their existence, let alone secure grant aid. So I was lucky, and indeed, it was luck in those bitter days, to be offered the job of Leader at a newly opened Girls' Club in Buxton at £90 per annum plus a flat. The club was designed to cater for homesick wenches who had been offered jobs in local hotels as part of a programme for the relief of unemployment of the young. Poor young things, as importees from coal-mining families in Derbyshire and the North East of England, they found it hard to adjust from the closeknit society of a mining community, to the reserved atmosphere of the ghetto of the elderly rich which Buxton then constituted.

Together we rambled on the hills. We danced to a wind-up gramophone, me always as a leading partner because boys were not permitted on the premises. We ate cheap chocolate biscuits and drank endless tea in the tiny canteen, which we ran on idealistic principles of common trust, until I discovered that the members had no compunction about helping themselves. They certainly taught me the facts of life. We were mutually astonished. Years afterwards, as a magistrate, I realised how much I owed to the confidences of a high-stepping Geordie whose escapades with a married man were something I had never even imagined before.

The club was in a high Victorian terrace house on the bleak marketplace. I lived in conscious independence in a flat on the top floor. Though I enjoyed it, the work was hard. Never mind having a degree and being middle-class, in the eyes of my committee of charitable ladies I was a paid employee and therefore automatically a social inferior. I was only summoned to join their meetings as and when required, till I acquired the technique of keeping my cards close to my chest, so that they found it impossible to conduct their business without my presence. Even so, a club leader was only a cut above a superior house-servant and they saw nothing wrong in loading on to me a spread of work that was beyond what any single human being could undertake, let alone one who prided herself on being a professional worker. In addition to running the club, I stoked the boiler in the basement, did some of the cleaning, all the administration and had to provide a bed and food for any stray girl brought in by the police at any hour of the day or night. I had never heard of venereal disease.

Little wonder that I was easily seduced by an ambitious woman who, in 1931, as Chairman of the Manchester and Salford Union of Girls' Clubs, persuaded me to accept the job of being its Organising Secretary. This was a single-sex organisation of course: the very idea of mixed clubs was regarded as near-scandalous. Single-handed, I was supposed to draw together the work of girls' clubs over a vast territory which stretched from Rochdale to Buxton, including Manchester and Salford. Every night, I was out and about in my empire. Social workers did not have cars in those days, though public transport was perhaps more adequate. There were works' clubs in good premises, organised by the new species of professional women personnel managers. There were large clubs run by old-established Missions-to-the-poor in the slums. Struggling little groups met in church halls, led by earnest ladies from the congregation. It was the hey-day of the girls' club movement. We wreaked havoc in the marriage market by educating our members away beyond the level of what the local man-power could produce. We were very much a spinster movement, pioneers of applied emancipation.

By day, I shared an office with the secretary of the Young Women's Christian Association (YWCA)—a little attic above the workrooms of a furrier in Manchester's smart King Street, poking away at a cast-off typewriter of such vintage that the type was set on a rotating barrel. I prepared agendas, wrote letters, organised competitions and festivals. Above all, I raised my own salary. My Committee consisted of stalwarts from the constitutional suffrage movement, two splendid Pilkington daughters amongst them. I lived at first at the University Settlement in the Round House at Ancoats, where people of the calibre of L. S. Lowry were to be encountered, but it cost £2 weekly and my total income was under £3. I moved to a house near the University in Victoria Park, where a Miss Guppy let out single rooms with the shared use of the kitchen to six of us, all single women of course. I drove myself harder and harder. I lived on less and less, learning where you got most value for money; the best buy was a plate of cowheel stew for ten old pence with unlimited free bread. It could not last and eventually I retreated to my long-suffering family and took to my bed to recuperate.

Duly recovered, I knew that I would be fortunate to get even temporary work by way of easing myself back into the swim of things. Like some damnable magnetic pole, chronic unemployment sucked into its orbit the whole energy of every charitable agency regardless of what might have been its original purpose. The Men's University Settlement, for example, led the local response to the appeal by the Prince of Wales for community centres for unemployed men. The first such club in Liverpool was the Number One Service Club which opened in Grafton Street down by the docks in 1931.

A more difficult situation in which to launch what was in intention an experiment in social regeneration, can hardly be imagined. Right from the start, every effort was made to delegate responsibility to the members, since it was properly realised that, however benevolent the management, to be reduced to the status of a dependent must inevitably contribute yet further to the destruction of self-respect caused by the mere fact of being out of work. But many of the men were the products of a long-standing tradition of casual labour on the docks from which the exercise of social responsibility had been largely omitted. Eventually eleven clubs were opened, catering for some two thousand members but, by and large, the desperate problems of the immediate distress so dominated current thinking that the lessons to be learned from the experiment were crowded out of mind. Arguments and quarrels were frequent and there was a general feeling that all that had been achieved was to move the street corner under cover.

Characteristically, as I was to learn, it was Josephine Duckworth, a leading figure in the girls' club world, who refused to accept that what could be said of unemployed men must automatically be true of unemployed women and girls. Perhaps what was commonly interpreted as failure was an indication that the fault lay in what was provided rather than the users?

Joey Duck, as she was affectionately called, had been a student at the School of Social Science who, in 1919, was appointed as the first full-time Secretary of the Union of Girls' Clubs through the initiative of D'Aeth. Her appointment was the outcome of the fact that, as she described it to me in a personal letter:

> during the 1914–18 war, a sufficiently large number of young people made themselves such a nuisance to their elders as to focus public attention on them. This was known among those same elders and the public as an Outbreak of Juvenile Crime, and it concerned the police and therefore the Home Office. What an indictment of society that it only became aware of youth when youth became a nuisance.

This led to the setting up in each big city of a Juvenile Organisations' Conference ('how you hate being called a Juvenile' was Joey's sharp rejoinder) which was to draw together all the agencies concerned with young people.

However, Joey was an instinctive democrat. She sensed danger in the development of what looked to her like state 'interference' whether in the shape of grants or by the actual provision of services. To her, even the tiniest group of girls, meeting in shoddy backstreet premises under the leadership of some 'superfluous' woman nevertheless had a certain inalienable right to mind their own business which no administrative pressure for tidiness must be permitted to infringe, no proffering of cash to undermine. Joey stoutly resisted D'Aeth's efforts to impose a tidy bureaucratic ceiling on the age of membership at 18, because it was imposed from above and was not based on the needs and wishes of the club itself.

> It had nothing to do with the (LUGC) whether a club stands on its head all night or says its prayers all night. And I would add that it has still less to do with the new partners of the club movement, the State and the Local Authorities. If either the Union or the State thinks it has, they must think again. Here is the seat of freedom. (Personal letter)

Refusing to accept the common assumptions, Joey set out to discover, by practical experiment, what unemployed women and girls really wanted or needed. I was duly appointed as project organiser, the grant for my salary coming from the LCVS but responsibility for the scheme remaining firmly with Joey. For lack of any other idea, we started off with a programme of classes in six centres in subjects we thought suitable for the unemployed. Part-time teachers were engaged, and I bravely descended on the queues at the Leece Street Labour Exchange and elsewhere, handing out little leaflets inviting women to one or other of the centres where classes were to be held. The girls no doubt regarded my approaches as a moment's relief from boredom but other response there was none, and few turned up at the meetings. Accordingly, we cut our programme down to size, and focused our efforts on three clubs only, one in the notorious Bull Ring housing estate in the inner city (only now being redeveloped) and two on new estates. Single-handed, all I could offer was physical training (not for nothing had I been to a public school) and cookery, my star turn being five ways of cooking a herring, one of which was to fry the fish in a biscuit tin lid over a paraffin stove. My friends thought me brave, not for trying to teach, but because I ventured alone into the big housing estates at Dovecot and Norris Green which were then passing through the horrors of initial settlement.

Then came the pain and the grief, as I struggled to write up the lessons of my six months' stint. All the deficiencies of my years of education were brought mercilessly out into the light of day. I was not capable of original thought. I chattered away entertainingly enough about what I had seen and done, but what did I, as an individual, think? What lessons had been learned? Poor Joey, how she wrestled with me. But to some effect because, when the report was published, it was favourably reviewed in a leader in the *Manchester Guardian* in May 1933, which actually mentioned me by name. The young man who was to become my husband and who was actively involved with the Number One Service Club, read their review and took a fancy to me there and then, I later discovered.

The gist of what I had to say was simply that the unemployed did not regard themselves as a category apart and resented being treated as such. That was valuable enough—it is a lesson we have still not learned sixty years on—but what was of far greater significance was the fact that I had stumbled on the quite desperate need for women to get together. Their wants were not catered for. Alienated and unwanted, in no way could they feel that they belonged to the community in which they found themselves. Shrewd politicking on the part of the breweries had ensured that there were at least pubs for men but for women, not even shops were always available. There was no place for them. The lesson I still had to learn was that my sage observation applied as much to me and my kind as to those labelled as unemployed.

For me personally, opportunity came in the shape of the Townswomen's Guilds, which were designed to carry forward the work of political education started by the Women Citizens' Association. Modest finance being made available through the LCVS, Janet McCrindell had secured for herself the job of organiser for the area, together with my services as secretary-housekeeper. Janet had been one of the first women to acquire a certificate as a Lady Sanitary Inspector. She subsequently acted as D'Aeth's lieutenant in promoting the Guilds of Help before becoming warden of the large girls' club associated with the Men's University Settlement. She had inherited a vast family house in one of those rather splendid Victorian streets which are such a feature of inner Liverpool. Here she took in as boarders a number of professional women who were by way of being pioneers in pursuing equal opportunities as lawyers, house property managers and so on. I typed her letters, dealt with callers, answered the phone and ran the house with the assistance of a comic-cuts daily whom we called Maybelle. The house hived with visitors.

It is not easy to express the happiness of that first experience of emancipation on the part of that little community of women. For those who had grown up in a working class tradition where it was taken for granted that women would work, the wider opportunities offered by the post-war period were welcome but not particularly startling. But for middle class young women like us, the vast expansion of our horizons was intoxicating. For such men as we met, it was perhaps a novel experience to meet women on this basis. For us women, it was both exhilarating and bewildering. We were first-generation female academics, first-generation 'professional' women, the first generation of middle class women to lead lives independent of our families. The first ever to escape—or so we thought—from compulsory domesticity.

When the franchise was at last extended to include all women in 1928, it symbolised for us the reality of our emancipation. The Women Citizens organised a grand Public Dinner by way of celebration, at which a toast—several toasts—were drunk in port, perhaps the explanation of the fact that when we came out into the streets to go home, even the shops and offices seemed to be dancing with joy. Not that we who were young, comprehended the magnitude of our inheritance. Like homing pigeons released in some strange land, we wheeled and circled, testing the dimensions of our new found freedom, searching to discover some sense of direction, some solid ground of values, in the chaotic aftermath of the war. We revelled in the fact that we stood for a new breed of women, blithely unaware of the fact that our appearance on the scene was to have repercussions that would echo on down the century till now they challenge the very foundations on which our social system has for so long depended.

Paradoxically enough, our sense of superiority as professionals over our lay colleagues did not dim the esteem in which 'voluntaryism' as a principle continued to be held. A social worker in a statutory service might be every bit as dedicated as any member of the staff of a voluntary agency, but the source of her salary, and perhaps its size, were automatically assumed to deprive her of some indefinable but essential moral attribute. As long as the employing agency could lay claim to being 'voluntary', the question of whether staff were paid workers or volunteers was not of relevance. The mystique of voluntaryism was ill-defined but doggedly maintained, often at considerable sacrifice on the part of paid staffs of voluntary agencies who were well accustomed in times of stringency to working at a reduced rate of pay, and, on occasion, without it.

For this reason, it mattered tremendously that we should still be able to believe that the agency which employed us was a charitable one. The label endowed us with a sense of self-sacrifice which was manna to our sometimes shaky self-esteem. The more overworked we were, and the less adequate our pay, the better for our morale. Even if we could afford nice clothes, we deliberately underplayed our attractions. We flaunted our social worker hats—usually a squashed and shabby felt—as a symbol of our dedication. In any case, to dress badly was a repudiation of the convention that women existed to please men.

This commitment to voluntaryism sat uneasily with the ever-increasing advance of the statutory services. It is hard to realise now, with bureaucrats in their thousands a commonplace of daily life, just what a fantastic monster the State appeared to us to be. We were still trying to digest the idea of paid social workers, people who actually took money for doing good; that a state employee should be regarded as a social worker was so alien to charitable tradition that it almost defeated comprehension. We regarded the onward march of the cohorts of the statutory services with a medley of instinctive hunch, moral principle and plain apprehension which is unbelievable today. We were illogically convinced of the moral superiority of being 'voluntary' even though we were ourselves paid workers and envious though we were of the salaries and security enjoyed by those employed by the state. One of the residents in McCrindell's establishment was an inspector of schools—and we eyed her with astonished curiosity because she found it possible at the same time to be a civil servant and a practising church-goer. We were deeply suspicious of any form of official intervention especially if it came in the shape of grant aid, as constituting a threat to our liberty and to our morals. Yet we could see no alternative to handing an increasing proportion of the burden of providing for the well-fare of the people to the State.

As we walked from one to another of the week-end cottages in the Clwyd Hills which it was then the fashion for academics to maintain, we debated and we argued. Endlessly we wearied on at conferences and seminars over the question of our relationship with the State. 'The Rôle of the Voluntary Worker': 'Voluntary Work and the Statutory Services': 'The Social Services and the Volunteer'—these were all variations on a single theme. How to counter the threat to the freedom of the individual—our precious freedom that we had fought so hard to secure—of this voracious monster, the State? The battle was much more equal then, of course. In 1933, the Personal Service Society claimed to have 450 voluntary workers, the Child Welfare Association, 500 and the Liverpool City Mission, 1000 (*Liverpool Quarterly*, 1933).

There was, however, yet another ingredient in the complex of pressures to which we were subjected that was of particular relevance to the middle class daughter such as myself. Our situation was one which I doubt is comprehensible in the 1990s except in terms of fiction. Ours was a world of women. At student dances, there would be quite literally, no men at all. Carr Saunders was a rare and god-like creature in our galaxy. Apart from him, we were taught by women with the exception of the aged Professor Mair Alexander, who sought to introduce us to the elements of both philosophy and psychology in six lectures, much of which he spent in private meditation, stroking his long white beard. When we went out to do our 'practical work', we were supervised by women. Eleanor Rathbone was able to gather about her no less than thirty 'apprentices', all unmarried, all looking to social work in some form or other as a panacea for their superfluity. 'Many have joined our ranks', noted Dorothy Keeling sadly, 'in order that they might find solace for some trouble of their own'.

Though we would have stoutly denied it, our failure to live up to society's expectations gloomed over our whole lives. It bred in me a life-long sensitivity to the injustice suffered by those who stand condemned for some 'fault' which is not of their own making. There simply were not enough men to go round. To us, bound hand and foot by the tradition of permanent mating as the proper career for women, there was no escape from the consequences. We were celibate by brute force of circumstance. The burden was made doubly hard to bear by the incessant repetition of music hall jokes about 'Superfluous Women'. Crudely put, but well we knew it to be true. I and others like me were literally superfluous to society's requirements.

Imagine then the enormous relief of encountering women like Eleanor Rathbone, Dorothy Keeling or dear Joey Duck, who seemed to have evolved a most satisfactory theory and practice of spinsterhood as a way of life, which visibly maintained their self-esteem even if the society in which they lived still treated them with patronage and pity. And what was more, their philosophy was not just a reaction to an unpalatable but inescapable necessity, but a calculated and fundamental doctrine of the forgetfulness of self in the service of the community as the very purpose of life itself. There was, of course, in those days no whisper of a suggestion of lesbianism. I doubt if many of us even knew the meaning of the word; we would certainly have been scandalised at any suggestion that the women we so greatly admired could have been guilty of what would then have been regarded as an impropriety. Our celibacy was essentially platonic.

One other issue remained to haunt us: the deeply unmentionable conflict between the natural inclination to seek marriage and motherhood, and the implication that this must necessarily be at the cost of our independence. The feminine dilemma of the future was only just beginning to make itself felt. For myself, I opted for marriage without a thought when my chance came, and retreated to the suburbs at the command of mother-in-law, thinking my independence well lost for the compensation of the companionship of the man of my choice.

Chapter 6
THE MACHINERY
OF GOVERNMENT

In which my appreciation of the importance of sound administration as the basis upon which the new relationship between society and individual must depend is strengthened by experience in the West Indies. I encounter for the first time the realities of the feminine dilemma.

All this fun and games, all-girls-together stuff ended abruptly after I married in 1935. Odd that I should have had to retire into the semi-contemplative life of the suburbs in order to arrive at an understanding of the first principles of life in a society. As was then customary for married women, I retreated to the far suburbs to spend my days keeping the house clean to a ridiculous standard; the gulf between domestic and professional life was pretty well total. I have been a kept woman ever since then. As the house was spit new, the cleaning of it amounted to very little: even allowing for polishing acres of wood block floors, every week of the year, the day's work petered out by ten o'clock. Fearsome hours stretched ahead which had to be filled with gardening and jamming and bottling. It is hard to believe how much time went on my husband's socks, knitting them, washing them, darning them. The boredom of it, the excruciating self-destroying boredom of it all. Caring for two adults (my son was not born till three years later) with one of them out of the house from half past eight in the morning till half past nine at night earning the mortgage, just could not absorb all the mental energies of an active young woman. I tried to find voluntary work locally but there was not enough of that to go round in our well-heeled suburb. I could fill in time well enough, but to what purpose?

As my husband settled to the task of producing the obligatory academic work necessary if he was to surmount the promotion hurdle, I found escape from my own futility in helping to revise the manuscript and correct the proofs of his *Principles of Social Administration* (London, Oxford University Press, 1937). Starting from the assumption that the social needs of the people of a modern society could only be met by universal provision, he argued the case for a sound system of administration as an absolute essential for good government. It was a conviction he shared with Elizabeth Macadam who had by this time left Liverpool but whom he encountered in her capacity as secretary of the Joint Universities Council for Social Services and Public Administration.

For my husband, the future lay in strengthening local government against the centralisation which was even then provoking apprehension. When, after a sad saga of trial and error, responsibility for the relief of the unemployed was finally taken over by the State, he was one of the rare few who observed that though there was considerable enthusiasm for control to be exercised over local activities by central government, too little thought was being given to the issue of ensuring that there was at the same time a counter-balancing increase in local control over central government. With remarkable prescience, he arrived at the conclusion that the dilemma between the retention of individual social responsibility and the delegation of power to the bureaucracy could only be resolved if the two worked together in partnership. This was the subject of his book. The implications were far reaching; it meant no less than that the traditional relationship between government and governed must be developed to an extent hitherto unknown in this country. From which he concluded that:

> ... If democracy is to rest on a secure foundation, much more must be expected from the citizen than a mere casting of his vote at election times. The details of administration, just as much as the drama of parliamentary debate, must be commonplaces of the discussion. Public administration must not be allowed to become a mystery, known only to the chosen few, or be carried on by a superior or privileged class of persons. (ibid., p. 157)

Nevertheless their enthusiasm did not blind them to the possible implications of what they were advocating. Macadam, for example, accepted as a regrettable necessity the fact that the kind of high-powered administration which she advocated must inevitably be conducted at a level which would exclude many of the general public: the rank and file of citizens, however well intentioned, had in her opinion neither the experience nor the capacity for involvement in such undertakings as the Merseyside Survey.

Though I never thought of my participation in all their discussions as anything more than a blessed escape from boredom, those years were in fact a far more relevant training for the life I was eventually to lead than all the courses I had soldiered through at the university.

This was no ivory-towered day-dreaming. The students who joined the course to acquire the newly established Diploma in Public Administration saw to that. Mature men and women with a fund of Lancashire wit and wisdom, they had an invaluable grasp of the realities of political life gained from their daily occupation in local government offices all over the north-west. What it was all about was, of course, the setting up of the scaffolding of the Welfare State though Beveridge was yet to come.

Not that there was anything that I could do to put my new-found enthusiasm into practice, trapped as I was in a web of domesticity. (I still remember the chill cast over my soul when I heard myself refuse my husband's invitation to sit-in on a new course of lectures that he was to give every Monday morning for the pitiful reason that that was my washing day.) Instead I had to be content with involvement at second-hand through my husband's close association with the LCVS. This had come about because as a resident at the University Settlement when he first arrived in Liverpool, he had been caught up in the affairs of the Service Clubs for the unemployed and consequently with the LCVS. Though the dead weight of unemployment still dominated all our lives, the take-over by the state in 1934 of responsibility for the subsistence of the unemployed had set people free to look about them and consider what other issues demanded attention.

The change of name from Liverpool Council of Voluntary Aid to Liverpool Council of Voluntary Service was significant of the change of attitude. Actively backed by the powerful business community, and with an invigorating input by the School of Social Science, the tradition of the 'New Testament' began to live again. The LCVS became an increasingly effective 'third force' in government, both locally and nationally. Conferences were held, training courses organised. *The Liverpool Quarterly*, of whose lively editorial board my husband was a member, was frankly propagandist, openly campaigning for constructive planning and attracting widespread attention.

One issue of particular concern was the dismaying realisation that re-housing was by no means the panacea for all ills that had been anticipated. A good house did not necessarily result in a good life. Spontaneously, tenants had begun to organise themselves into groups and by 1934, there were as many as twenty Tenants' Associations scattered about the outer suburbs. Sturdy and aggressive, many of them women, these were a very different kettle of fish from the Institutes of D'Aeth's original intention. In an attempt to meet the situation, the existing LCVS Community Committee was replaced by a New Estates Committee, but the mix of activist tenants and representatives of the established agencies was an uneasy one. Tenants as voluntary workers were a species not previously encountered in the charitable scene.

Unhappily the jockeying for position between Liverpool Corporation as landlords and citizens as tenants developed into an on-going confrontation that alienated interest in the demand for the provision of community facilities. On the other hand, there was considerable support for what was officially called The Service of Youth from which the community centre movement incidentally benefited. Even so, everyone was tired after the long struggle to survive the endless years of the depression. Social problems of immense difficulty remained to be resolved. In such circumstances, the need for the provision of centres for community life took a low priority.

I skirmished rather ineffectually on the fringes of all this. The birth of my son in 1937, though immensely gratifying, made it even more difficult for me to do anything more than make occasional contributions to conferences or write articles for local newsletters. My husband bore my thrashing about with commendable fortitude, but I became increasingly frustrated. I knew that I was an indifferent housewife and a poor mother, but there seemed to be no alternative.

However, an unlooked for new dimension was added to my existence by reason of the fact that through Macadam, my husband had inevitably come to know Eleanor Rathbone. It was impossible to know the one without being involved in the concerns of the other.

Eleanor, having won the election as representative of the Combined Universities in 1929, was then becoming known as the Member of Parliament for Refugees. My husband consequently found himself caught up in the drive to persuade the Universities to sponsor the entry into this country of Jewish colleagues at risk in Germany and Austria. He managed to secure the appointment to his Department, of which he was made Professor in 1937, of a woman psychologist from Vienna, a refugee from Hitlerism. Through her, by what was to become a familiar progression, we became closely involved with other members of her family. My husband being Chairman of the Merseyside Co-ordinating Committee, our house rapidly became the focus for the welfare of refugees in the whole area. All the more so after the arrival of Hertha, 'our refugee', a particularly charming young woman from Vienna, who quickly developed the rôle and reputation of an all-purpose welfare officer for refugees throughout Merseyside.

The relationship between hosts and guests was often a difficult one. University wives, who tended to be essentially suburban, thought that they were employing a domestic help, even though on compassionate grounds. What they encountered were highly professional men and women who were socially their equals and often intellectually their superiors. I was shocked to learn that refugees valued a visit to us because ours was the only house where they were given tea in the sitting room and not the kitchen—and out of a silver teapot! Perhaps the horror of the stories our guests had to tell was beyond the understanding of many people, and the torrent of emotion with which it was expressed was often alien to a suburban setting.

Contact with our refugee friends enormously extended our comprehension of the sense of community from which their strength derived and our profound respect for the capacity of human beings to survive the loss of all that might be thought to make life worth living. But ours was by no means a common experience. What did make a much more general impact was the arrival on our own doorsteps of children evacuated from the inner city on the outbreak of war in 1939.

Filled with emotion, as were so many others, we hurriedly cleared our dining room—then an essential for decent suburban living—of its formal furnishings, its sideboard and its silver, its neat array of chairs round a shining mahogany table, and fitted it up as accommodation for a mother and child. Instead we were allocated an entire family of young children and their mother plus a father who came for weekends. They came from the dockside area of Scotland Road and the children could talk of little other than a domestic murder with which they were somehow connected. Though I was familiar enough with poverty through going to the Victoria Settlement, to live cheek-by-jowl with a family reared to a life of multi-deprivation was a stunning revelation. We managed to get on quite well so far as sharing the cooker and the kitchen sink went, but there was a gulf between us a mile wide. How much more so for my neighbours, few of whom had ever before encountered 'the poor' at such close quarters. We struggled along, but our particular little family found suburban living too dismal an experience to be endurable—a sentiment with which I heartily agreed—and along with many others, they headed back for the city.

There can be no doubt that this first-hand encounter with a way of life which no civilised society could accept was a major factor in preparing the ground for the Beveridge Plan announced in 1941 while the war was still on. However the smug assumption that support for the idea of a Welfare State sprang from some great surge of compassion for the deprived glossed over a much more complex and disturbing truth. Pity there certainly was but also an ominous sense of revulsion. However guilty the Haves might feel about the Have-nots, certainly little love was lost between the two. The poor were objects of charity, not affection. Significantly, an examination of the evacuation scheme by my husband's Department together with the LCVS, appeared under the title *Our Wartime Guests—Opportunity or Menace?* (1940). This was an attempt to assess the extent to which evacuation had led to a weakening of the social ties which bound the community together rather than the reverse.

> When it [the scheme] has broken down—as it undoubtedly has so far as multitudes both of hosts and guests are concerned—it is not unlikely that the horror felt by so many of the middle classes who were confronted by what they considered to be the dirty habits of the slum people in their own homes, and the disgust felt by slum people who suffered what they felt was cold and inhuman treatment from their hosts, will lead to a weakening of the social ties which bind the community together, rather than the reverse.

Yet contrariwise, out of the shared dangers which were much more widely experienced than in the First World War, there developed a camaraderie which cut across all the customary distinctions between men and women, class and class. My husband, for example, who was very much a Balliol philosopher, derived enormous pleasure from the company of a mixed bag of fire-watchers who shared with him the boiled black puddings which sustained them through long dark nights. Again, a wealthy spinster cousin who had been reared to social superiority found herself in charge of a group of fast-living young women called up for army service. She became so involved with them that she adopted three of the offspring of their adventures. High hopes were indulged that the growing awareness of social solidarity would provide the basis for the building of a better society after the war.

It felt like running away when, early in 1941 as the blitz on Liverpool was nearing its peak, we sailed off down the Mersey to the West Indies. Until then, we had had a pretty average sort of war, my husband drafted to a succession of dreary civil service jobs in London. I stayed at home with my tiny offspring, fretting at my futility, my only relief being the organisation in what had been our dining room of what must have been one of the first Play Groups on Merseyside. We refused a chance for me to go with our son to the States; if there was any dying to be done, we would all die together.

Then came this astonishing invitation to go out to the West Indies. I could barely distinguish between the East and the West Indies at that stage. There had been unusually widespread disturbances right across the Caribbean in

1937 and a Royal Commission had been sent out to investigate. Lord Moyne, the Chairman, and his colleagues had toured the islands in his private yacht but the plutocratic impression that conveyed was corrected by the production of a forthright report. The gist of it was that conditions in the West Indies were disgraceful and urgently called for the application of a programme for development and welfare. Nothing had ever been done to replace the discredited plantation economy of the previous century.

I doubt if these recommendations would have received quite such a prompt response but for the fact that American troops at the Caribbean bases provoked a threat of renewed trouble by attempting to exclude black people from using the local swimming pools. As it was, Sir Frank Stockdale was promptly appointed as Comptroller for Development and Welfare in the West Indies, given a bag of gold and a team of experts to advise him on how to spend it, and sent out to 'keep the natives quiet'. My husband was reluctant to agree to what seemed a soft option but eventually accepted appointment as Social Welfare Adviser. We were given to understand that my experience as a youth worker would be valued.

The team of Advisers once assembled in Trinidad, the first move was to set out on a Grand Tour of the territory covered by the remit of what quickly became known as the Stockdale Circus. We paused in each island, sometimes for months, to get the hang of the local situation and make contacts with local people. Trinidad to Jamaica, with stops-off in Venezuela and Bogota, then on to the Leewards and the Windwards, by way of Cuba and Haiti. And so to Antigua and Barbados, lovely, peaceful, poverty-stricken Barbados. Then on again to Trinidad and so back to Jamaica. The official members of the party were able to use military transport but the rest of us—the other wives and me and my small son—trailed along behind as and when opportunity offered.

It was a quite extraordinary experience to go from the shattered Liverpool of the blitz to the full fig of the Colonial Empire. After the comradeship of wartime Britain, we found it impossible to accept the excessive respect and servility which was accorded to us as members of the white official class. Our Englishness was emphasised at every turn. We were given prunes for breakfast, brought at vast risk to life across the seven seas, although grapefruit lay rotting on the ground all about us. We dressed for dinner at Government House, struggling to put on shoulder length white kid gloves of which I had seven pairs, given to me by a friend who in her girlhood had been an Edinburgh debutante. Official life was strictly ruled by custom and habit. It was not permissible to sample the chocolates in their silver dishes—a rare treat to us, of course—till after we had drunk the health of His Majesty, saluting a rather indifferent portrait of Him as we did so. We were bemused to observe modest civil servants from the minor suburbs of England, accepting as to the manner born the services of black men dressed up as flunkeys. We consumed, apparently without compunction, large meals served to us by domestics whose rates of pay were little above starvation level. No wonder there was a yale lock on our 'fridge.

We quickly resolved that all that Empire bit was totally foreign to us. Driven by the memory of the savagery of the blitz, there could be for us no sitting around in rocking chairs on verandahs, drinking rum punch. Abandoning the luxury of such tourist hotels as were still available, we settled for the discomforts of a random succession of rented houses where we could lead our own kind of life and meet our own kind of friends. There had been no butler in our previous existence and we saw no reason why we should acquire one now. We reduced our domestic staff to a minimum to whom we paid the wages we would otherwise have spread over a half dozen or so. We gave the keys of the 'fridge to the cook, aghast at the prospect of a relationship with her based on such deep mistrust.

What we found so peculiarly galling was the strict embargo on any kind of informal social contact with local black people. There were we, cut off from home, starving for books to read and well informed people to talk to. And there were people whose houses overflowed with books, who not only had a stock of records but were themselves highly expert musicians, widely travelled, well educated, leading lives of a sophistication far beyond anything we had known in our provincial suburb or was available to us in official circles. When we ignored the embargo, those in authority took us aside and first advised and then threatened that our behaviour could have serious consequences. There was clearly no future for a man like my husband in the cabined and confined structure of the Colonial Office, a blond senior civil servant advised me earnestly.

My husband's North Country directness which so distressed gubernatorial circles, as they were pompously called, was an asset in meeting black people who had rarely experienced such treatment at the hands of a white official. Rapidly we learned to look the black man in the face instead of averting our gaze. Without realising what was happening, we became so acclimatised to a multiracial society that we no longer noticed the physical composition of our company.

The Royal Commission had commented on the enthusiasm of the people they encountered for discussion of their problems, and on their understanding and forward-looking attitude towards them. Sure enough, once it was clear that we were genuinely open to meet all and sundry, our only difficulty was how to fit into our days the vast range of visits and interviews pressed upon us. We rose earlier and earlier and worked harder and harder, hareing all across Jamaica in the heat and dust to visit some remote land settlement, driving up and down the length and breadth of Trinidad, luxuriating in the sweet coolness of Barbados, entranced by the historical associations of Antigua. We met all and sundry from potential Prime Ministers to unknown doers of good who struggled to run a troop of Boy Scouts in some backwater. We inspected prisons, and workhouses, youth clubs and land settlements. We ran conferences and training courses which served to lay the foundations of the University of the West Indies. We met black and white and all varieties in between. We talked with Asians and Chinese, Catholic priests, Salvation Army troopers and Methodist ministers. It made a splendid story and we had to guard against becoming known as the Great West India Bores when we returned to Liverpool.

For all that we had been so deeply interested in plans for the coming of the welfare state in Britain and so concerned as to the part to be played by the ordinary person in building a new society, the atmosphere in a provincial university could hardly be described as revolutionary. Whereas the entire length and breadth of the whole chain of islands from Jamaica right down to Trinidad was ablaze with the demand for independence from Colonial rule. In a gale of exuberance, people in every island fell to inventing from scratch the principles and practice of building a community. On the basis of the remnants of colonial tradition and the fading memories of the formalised cooperation of the African tribe, they set themselves to build a new society and educate its people to a democratic way of life they had never before experienced. Not least, they had to work out for themselves a relationship between government and governed specifically geared to the novelty of the long-awaited achievement of independence.

The pious sentiments we had habitually uttered at conferences at home about 'the universal right to social responsibility' took on a startling relevance when set in the context of a people struggling to escape from the tradition of slavery. The vigour of their commitment to freedom, the vitality of the enterprise with which they set about implementing it, above all the gaiety of their companionship constituted a revelation of the meaning of the words we had so frequently used. Community, social structure, social responsibility above all, justice: over and over again we were forced by the reality of experience to redefine our own terms of reference.

Not that the going was ever easy. We met poverty, literal starvation—

poverty such as we had never thought possible. Where every prospect pleased and only man was vile, the price was being paid for man's cruelty to man. There was aggression and antagonism to overcome, a hard task with a bitter tradition of slavery behind us and colonialism solid all about us still. There was the forbidding immensity of the economics of the situation. The fortunes of all the islands depended on sugar cane and bananas and both industries were in decline. Rum was too cheap and food too dear. There was apathy and sloth and ill-health and ignorance and straight obstruction from both black and white with vested interests. This was a rootless society without a common culture, looking to a future which seemed to be without prospect. And the 'Circus', with its annual dollop of money, had been set the task of creating out of all this a society fit and able to enjoy the paradise in which it was set down.

Gradually out of this whirl of activity some sense of direction began to emerge. The situation was that there was good neighbourliness galore but little trace of either the spontaneous coming together of people to 'get things done' which was taken for granted in England or, even more importantly, of the formalised cooperative activities of the African tribe. Thanks to Norman Manley, the great Jamaican patriot, it was Jamaica that took the lead in devising new methods of remedying this deficiency. Manley was the acknowledged leader of the independence movement throughout the West Indies, a man of impressive brilliance and vision.

After the troubles in 1937, Manley had persuaded the banana growers to pay a levy of a halfpenny on every bunch exported and with the funds thus raised, he set up Jamaica Welfare Ltd. This was a voluntary agency directed towards schemes for promoting 'the social and economic betterment of the working classes', mainly in the rural areas. However, it rapidly outgrew this benevolent intention. Based largely on the existing land settlement movement, a considerable programme developed on lines familiar to the cooperative movement in Europe where two of the workers had been sent for training. The introduction of tomato-growing in a particularly infertile area was an outstanding success and when we returned to England we were proud to see on the shelves of grocers' shops a selection of fruit juices produced under the label of Trout Hall.

The first attempts at the development of community life as distinct from individual welfare were less successful. Two expensive centres were built on European lines without much result; the gaunt ghost of the one at Porus was literally concrete proof of the futility of imposing an idea on an uncomprehending people who had themselves quite other ideas as to what should be done with any available money. That lesson learned, Jamaica Welfare set to with zest on devising alternative ways and means of stimulating a feeling of social awareness in people whose lives were dominated by their individual struggle for survival. In the process, the basic principles of community development were whacked out. Social change would not come about by the provision of any single service; the essence of it lay in the interaction of social, economic and political forces. What use teaching a man to read and write if he had no food in his stomach or roof over his head and no means of acquiring them? This interaction alone would breed that spontaneous combustion essential for that which we call social change.

Out of trial and error there began to emerge a grasp of the principles and practice of community building that was far in advance of anything we had known before. It was for example not the provision of a church or school or centre that mattered, but the process of building it that was itself a contribution to the building of the community. Betterment would only result if 'felt needs' as the current cliché put it, percolated up and were not imposed from the top down. As Manley put it, people must be educated as agents of their own betterment, not 'improved' by direct provision from outside.

Seen in this light no project was too small or insignificant to be of value. Swept along by the enthusiasm and energy of Thom Girvan, the Director of Jamaica Welfare, all and sundry found themselves caught up in a remarkable spirit of unity (see D. T. M. Girvan, *Working Together*, Kingston, Institute of Jamaica, 1993). Boy Scouts, women's craft shops, folk song groups, Young Farmers' Clubs, churches, food projects, a literacy campaign, anybody and everybody began to grasp the possibility of a new and independent Jamaica. Oh, the fun and the laughter, the exuberant vitality, the scorching pace they set. And having no past that they cared to remember, with what hope and sweetness and forgiveness they eyed the future. This was a young country, forward looking. They had so much to give us. Not least there was the warmth of our mutual affection which was to be a perpetual inspiration in the fight against racism which, unbeknownst to us, lay waiting for us against the day of our return.

Manley was well aware that the policy he pursued was one which must in the long run involve a totally new relationship between government and governed. The issue was forced out into the open when submarine warfare moved from the Atlantic to the Caribbean. This brought the banana levy to an abrupt halt. My husband was deeply involved in the consequent negotiations designed to persuade the government to assume the responsibility for funding Jamaica Welfare without damaging its independence. The outcome was a quite remarkable contribution to the machinery of governance which was based not only on a close partnership between government, people and private enterprise but put their relationship on an administrative foundation which made for a novel blending of their respective contributions. Not only had the different services to be persuaded to co-operate with each other but they also had to accept the principle that as well as aiming to improve economic and social conditions, the programme must also include the development of political responsibility of the part of the community as a whole.

In the context of the rising demand for independence this was a bitter pill for the Colonial Service to swallow. The end product, as Manley intended, must be the death of colonialism and the birth of a new and independent Jamaica. My husband was reduced to extremes of cloak and dagger behaviour in his efforts to discuss the situation with local politicians, sneaking through a little back garden gate after nightfall in order to visit Manley. In the end, the Governor of Jamaica threatened to intern him as a subversive. We only escaped from the island at dawn one hot morning thanks to the assistance of a well-disposed official who surreptitiously secured an exit permit for us. It was a source of infinite gratification to us that when eventually Jamaica won its independence, my husband returned to the island as a personal guest of the new government.

What has become of all that gallant endeavour is a subject for sober reflection. Sadly enough, in the context of Toxteth fifty years on, I find myself recollecting that we came to the conclusion then that what was needed was not more missionaries *to* the West Indies but a mission *from* the Caribbean to Europe. The resurgent mood of the black communities in our inner cities today has everything to learn from the pioneers of the independence movement of their forbears.

Chapter 7
A VOLUNTARY WORKER
IN THE WELFARE STATE

In which, having achieved a satisfying life for myself as a voluntary
worker in the welfare state, I was jolted out of my complacency by
the realisation that nevertheless I was getting nowhere. I conclude
that sound administration alone is not enough; it must be fuelled
by the political will to act. I determine to become a City Councillor.

There was never any question of my settling down into suburban domesticity
after the astounding extensions of my horizons which I had experienced in
the West Indies. The war was still on. My husband was absorbed in writing his
book on *Welfare and Planning in the West Indies* (London, Oxford University Press,
1946) in the teeth of opposition from the Colonial Office, which tried to prevent his use of information acquired during his stint as an official. My son was,
educationally speaking, pretty well wrecked by having been to eleven schools
in five years, so he went off to St Christopher's at Letchworth, which made a
remarkably good job of him and totally convinced me of the merits of a truly
comprehensive education. And a key factor, mother-in-law, who had moved
next door to oversee my child-rearing, had died. There was nothing to keep us
in the suburbs.

We sold our house, for six times what we paid for it, to a profiteer who
arrived with the cash in a suitcase, and we bought a house in the inner-city
area of Liverpool 8. Blackburne Terrace had been built for the up-and-coming
middle classes in 1826 but by the time we got there, it had become an enclave
of decaying respectability set in a sad slum. However, in addition to being
more or less untouched Regency, it had the merit of being just round the
corner from the University and within walking distance of everything that
mattered in the city centre.

I luxuriated in the sense of space after the constrictions of a modern house:
the draughty staircases, the high ceilings, the upstairs drawing-room with its
three tall windows. It felt like an expansion of my personality to have a room

of my own even if being wartime it was hard to acquire fittings and furniture to put in it. Wartime shortages and restrictions lingered on for years after 1945, making it difficult to restore our ark of a building to anything like minimum standards. We made good our deficiencies in the way of furniture for so large an establishment by forays round the local junk shops which were full of the debris of the blitz. There was no running water in the main building and the electric fittings had been stripped down to the last screw and switch. There were no door handles whatsoever. The house had been used as a hostel for overseas 'coolies' on the ships; they left it spotlessly clean but bereft of every detachable fitting. To this day, bits and pieces of 3 Blackburne Terrace must be scattered about the Far East. Even moving the furniture had to be a do-it-yourself effort; my husband used to take a load in the trailer every day when he went to the University.

The toil of running so large a house with only random domestic help was a revelation of what life must have been like for servants in Victorian times. Coals for the sitting-room fire had, for example, to be brought from a cellar under the front portico, lugged up the basement stairs, then up the main staircase to the first floor. It never struck me as curious that I, who had so bitterly resented what I regarded as the drudgery of domestic life in the suburbs should now take so happily to a far more demanding load of household chores. What made the difference was, of course, the vital change which the move to town brought about in our way of life. No more dismal weeding of the garden in isolation and loneliness except for the neighbour's dog. No more long hours to fill in while I waited for my husband's return in the evening. Minding the house was no longer the purpose of my life but its background.

Our lives as a married couple were transformed. My husband speedily developed the habit of bringing home with him either colleagues or students who wanted to pursue some conversation in more peace and quiet than the Department could provide. We installed an Aga. I fed visitors galore, catered for an endless stream of external examiners and visiting lecturers, including people of the magnitude of Richard Titmuss, Franklin Frasier and Margaret Mead. And in my spare time, I finished my book on *Charitable Effort in Liverpool in the Nineteenth Century* (op. cit.) which was published in 1951 as part of the University's contribution to the Festival of Britain. I look back in astonishment at it all. How on earth did one pair of hands ever achieve so much and with such good grace?

I was more than content that all this should be so. It simply never occurred to me that I should strike out on an independent career of my own. I took it for granted that my duties as a wife and mother, and as a daughter after my aged mother joined us, must have priority over any interests of my own and was only too happy to thrive on the crumbs that fell from my husband's table. A political career was something I never contemplated. 'Politics' were out for University wives, and to be honest, I suspect that I regarded politicians as a low order of being.

Nevertheless I was a product of my times and there was no escaping the sheer practicalities of the feminine dilemma. The literal conflict between fitting in my domestic obligations with the pursuit of my outside interests came to dominate my days. All about me other women were facing the same problem. We had sampled the freedom of life beyond the kitchen sink and few of us were willing to give it up for undiluted domesticity. For myself, I was singularly lucky in that the world I sought to enter overlapped with that of my husband so that we were actually drawn together by the very fact that I was beginning to launch out on my own. But many others were, and still are, less fortunate.

As 'Mrs Prof' I took it for granted that I would occupy myself with what was vaguely lumped together as 'voluntary work', voluntary presumably meaning that I did it without pay. Few academic wives worked for money in those days and I was a kept woman all my married life; my husband used to complain at intervals that it was his turn to stay at home and mine to go out and earn our living. As might be expected, I headed back for the Victoria Settlement, only to discover that life had moved on since last I had been there. The huge programme of legislation necessary for the implementation of the Beveridge Plan was very much the dominant issue of the day and as the various public services came into being, attention increasingly focused on the administration of benefits. The ensuring of an even-handed deal for every beneficiary became a matter of political and professional principle, so much so that all down the years ever since it has absorbed more and more attention and has given rise to the latest specialism of all, the welfare rights bureaux.

The rise of this new breed of bureaucratic philanthropist gave rise to universal confusion as to the rôle of voluntary workers in the expanding empire of the welfare state—if indeed, they had one at all. Beveridge's declaration of faith in voluntary action as the basic principle of democratic government was universally ignored. There seemed to be little scope for the amateur in the hierarchy of trained case-workers. The relief of those in need was no longer seen as the concern of the Settlement. The implementation of Beveridge and his Plan was the responsibility of the government. After the battering the neighbourhood had endured during the blitz, the urgent concern of local people was to restore something of the community life they had once enjoyed. Money was hard to come by other than for youth work. Our old building was sadly decrepit. All around us were the physical and social ruins of the aftermath of war. The whole thing was run on a shoe-string and looked like it. Our only asset was the do-it-ourselves spirit bred by the war.

Undeterred, we set about the transformation of our long-established system of management-by-patronage into one suited to a community-based Centre. There were endless meetings with all and sundry at which we thrashed out a new constitution. By 1947, we were ready and with a flourish of trumpets and in the presence of the Lord Mayor and Lady Mayoress, with their customary entourage of footmen and potted plants, we celebrated the Settlement's Golden Jubilee by boldly declaring our conversion into a community centre. The members responded valiantly and their enthusiasm offset the bickering which disfigured the relationship between members of the previous committee as we moved from one era to another. Nevertheless, it soon became evident that we had to have outside support, both financial and in terms of official recognition. Voluntary contributions and even the most dedicated service by voluntary workers, were simply not enough. I struggled on as Secretary for a while, then as Chairman, but what with the onset of slum clearance and the lack of official support, progress petered out and we began to lapse back into the habits of charitable tradition. Some other basis for promoting community development would have to be found. Unexpectedly, the Wavertree Centre came to our rescue.

The Wavertree Centre was by way of being a cuckoo in the nest of such of the community movement as had survived the war. It had originated in the fact that the LCVS was holding funds donated by Americans—already pacesetters in such activity—for community work in the city. Inevitably the lack of places for people to meet dominated the discussion as to what should be done with the money and eventually, after a maddeningly frustrating series of delays, a community centre was opened in 1946. This was in a large villa in Penny Lane, of later Beatles fame, selected because it had already been acquired by a Director of Education with empire-building tendencies. It stood in a residential neighbourhood and for the next ten years or so, flourished as a recreational and social club attracting a large membership of younger people as they returned to civilian life.

Comparisons were inevitable. The Wavertree Centre seemed to some of us to be unduly favoured with its paid staff and comfortably furnished building:

we all went there to watch the Coronation of the Queen on TV because so few of us then had access to a set. Visitors were proudly brought by officialdom to visit it as an example of community provision and this naturally provoked resentment amongst the impoverished centres in the inner city or on the housing estates that lacked even a roof under which to meet.

There was, however, one unexpected and highly significant by-product in that the Centre provided a meeting place for people from all over the city who were involved in community work but had never before come together to discuss their aims and problems. The conferences and meetings held at the Centre at week-ends began to attract city personalities and officials as well as the sometimes inarticulate committee members from the outer housing estates. They also drew in representatives from all manner of groups in white-collar suburbs who, being employed in the city centre and being people of greater experience, were able to visit the Education Office and other agencies in search of advice and support. Traditional centres, such as the Settlement which I represented, found ourselves increasingly regarded as has-beens from the past.

Gradually a head of steam was generated, though considerable confusion stemmed from the fact that no-one was clear as to what was the purpose of all this activity. The National Council for Voluntary Service had laid down guidelines as far back as 1937 for what was developing into a national movement, but in practice it was difficult to apply their distinction between a community association, as a cog in the machinery of local government like a parish council, and a community centre as a physical base from which to conduct its activities. How could an association flourish without somewhere to meet, yet having acquired premises, how could it be expected to look beyond the chronic problem of finding money to run them?

In an effort to be helpful, the LCVS created a Community Centres Council to take over from where the pre-war New Estates Council had left off. However, their customary mix of businessmen and representatives of the established organisations found it difficult to accommodate the frustration of grass roots members from the Centres who demanded action, not patronage. After many spirited wrangles, in which I was closely involved, the centres split off and in 1952 set up their own Federation of Community Centres, the steering committee of which met regularly in our dining-room in a conspiratorial atmosphere which was much enjoyed. More importantly, in the process, we discovered for ourselves by trial and error and limitless argument, the principles and practice of democracy.

Once launched into independence, the Federation grew in numbers and effectiveness, justifiably coming to be regarded as an example of excellence in what was rapidly becoming a national movement of which my husband became actively involved as President. In the early 1950s there were as many as seventeen Centres scattered about Merseyside.

It would have been easy to get bogged down in the daily crises at the Settlement and the long-running saga of the birth of the Federation. However, I was jolted out of that particular rut by the fact that in 1952 I was appointed as a magistrate on the Liverpool Bench. It is revealing of the gulf that separated voluntary work from the world of the establishment that I treated the rather scruffy letter inviting me to accept nomination with flippancy and actually had to retrieve it, unanswered, from the waste paper basket. I only accepted when it was pointed out to me that as one of a bunch of 'younger' men and women specifically appointed to stock up the Juvenile Bench—I was then 46—I might be able to promote a more sympathetic attitude to young delinquents. In the event, I came to enjoy it. The infinite variety of human behaviour was endlessly fascinating. It fulfilled my girlhood ambition to be a lawyer. And oh, the dizzy pleasure as a woman of being 'Your Worship', a person of consequence in my own right! When, by virtue of seniority it fell to me to occupy the chair at the major morning session, it was suggested by a male colleague that I might prefer to step aside in his favour. To his astonishment and certainly to my own, I firmly asserted my right to this responsibility.

Personal gratification apart, sitting in Court brought home to me what I had never before encountered in quite so stark a form, the gulf in mutual comprehension which separated those of us who took part in 'government' from those over whom we exercised authority. I was dumbfounded by the complacency with which their ignorance was accepted by the bulk of my colleagues with the glorious exception of Bessie Braddock, and was frequently on the brink of tears as I struggled at our pompous Quarterly Meetings in the Town Hall to challenge their assumption of superiority. More practically, because of my long involvement in youth work, it seemed to me obvious that there needed to be much closer cooperation between all the services concerned with young delinquents—probation, the police and school attendance officers. I laboured away at bringing to life a Joint Committee of all three and only learned with pain and grief what hidden obstacles obstructed the path to progress in that regard.

My appetite for public life must have been whetted by what it fed on because a year or so later, I accepted with some enthusiasm an invitation to serve as a coopted member of the Education Committee, the Labour Party having won the local elections for the first time ever in 1955. I was apprehensive about the extent to which I would have to toe the party line but who can resist patronage from on high? And after the decorum of the Bench, what joy unconfined to hear an Alderman shouted down with cries of 'Shut up, Joe. We've heard all that before'.

Education was a well-run department, dominated by a Director who was a Methodist lay preacher. He included the performance of the Councillors amongst his responsibilities and taught me that officers get the Committee they deserve. We had a Trojan woman as Chairman in Dame Ethel Wormald, resources were reasonably good and growth a realistic proposition. True to type, all my energies went into promoting what were called the support services, designed to ensure that all and sundry would be enabled to benefit from education in the broadest sense of the word. School meals, special schools for the physically and mentally handicapped, pre-school provision for all, youth clubs and such like became my speciality. I also joined in with spirit in the long running battle against the exclusiveness of the 11+ selection examination and the setting up of comprehensive schools.

Because of my experience as a Juvenile Court Magistrate, my particular interest was in school attendance. Early on, a cagey old Alderman had warned me against trying to intrude on the established territory of the big boys but to find some uncultivated corner for myself. Thanks to him, I discovered the School Attendance Service, the forgotten Cinderella of the Education Department, literally housed in the basement of a lovely Art Nouveau building. They were as surprised to encounter a committee member who was interested in their affairs as I was to come across a service which was committed to bridge-building between all the specialist departments involved in the care of children. Though they aspired to higher standards and status, and fought doggedly to win professional qualifications, they always typified for me my ideal of a 'civil service of the streets'. I vastly enjoyed their company. Many were Shakespearian characters in their own right, robust men and women with a strong sense of moral values. At that stage their only qualification was often that they had taught in a Sunday School and sang in a church choir. Certainly their performance of 'Blaydon Races' in a charabanc at the Whitley Bay conference was memorable. Their very special merit for me was that they were examples of that rare species, officials who bridged the gulf which separated specialism from specialism. They were essentially social workers, although they operated within the field of education: their remit comprised the police, probation officers and youth workers.

My other major interest was the youth and community service, largely the province of voluntary workers. Elizabeth Macadam had worked for years to institute a qualification for youth workers that would be universally recognised but this very necessary ambition was healthily countered in Liverpool by the strong tradition of voluntary action. Building on the foundations laid by D'Aeth in the 1920s, we eventually achieved the establishment of a Joint Organisations Committee (JOC) composed of representatives of the voluntary bodies, elected Councillors and officials in equal parts. Gradually the sheer utility of such a body for relieving the Education Committee of the burden of internecine quarrels, together with the competence with which its affairs were serviced by the officials, won for the JOC an increasing share of the responsibility for both policy-making and the dispensing of grants. It worked so well that on one occasion the Tory leader of the Council remarked that he might as well hand over the entire sum allocated to community work in the Annual Budget to the JOC and let them get on with it. Though the JOC enjoyed such broad responsibilities it was, of course, ultimately accountable to the Education Committee.

This was all well and good but the tide of circumstance flowed strongly against us. As the pressures of housing need climbed to crisis point, the hope that the building of houses would be complemented by the building of communities gave way to the quick-fix of multi-storey blocks of flats. All that mattered was to get roofs over the heads of desperate people, the huge bulk of whose need was of a dimension and an urgency beyond the comprehension of today. Moreover, surveys began to challenge the assumption basic to much planning, that people identified with the area in which they lived. The hope that community groups might become part of the machinery of local government faded from sight. Indeed, community work was firmly classified as recreational and therefore placed under the control of the Education Committtee; centres were specifically forbidden by the grant aid regulations from dabbling in either politics or religion.

Nevertheless, full of missionary zeal, I plodded on in the confidence that change could be achieved by patient persuasion: reason must surely triumph. Bad money might drive out good but good example must certainly be victorious over evil. At that stage I saw my modest role in terms of what we would now call networking. I myself described it as knitting up the fabric of a disintegrating society. The more I saw at first hand of the administration of services both statutory and voluntary, the more scandalised I became by the way in which each ran in its own specialist rut regardless of the needs of individuals as whole human beings, or of the communities they existed to serve. The gap between 'Them', the providers, and 'Us' the users was not only inefficient but seriously disturbing. Clearly there was something wrong with the system that produced it.

For all my running about from pillar to post, spinning my web of connections, it was gradually borne in on me that I was getting nowhere. Personally, I had achieved a gratifying status as a university wife, a magistrate, a twinset-and-pearls liberal. As a voluntary worker, I was quite a big fish in my little pond. What more did I want? Surveying the sum total of my activities, I had to admit that for all the satisfaction I derived from my efforts at bridge-building, the effect on the administration of the services was absolutely nil. Councillors and officials listened politely to my prattle but they knew, and gradually I came to realise that they knew, that as a coopted member of the Education Committee I was no more than committee fodder. I realise with hindsight that I was trying to feed new ideas into a machine that was by definition geared to the administration of what already existed. There was no room in it for the likes of me, a coopted member and voluntary worker. I had been turned into a reliable foot soldier, one of those dim members who toe the party line, never miss a meeting and suffer acutely from the utter ineffectiveness of their presence.

And of course, as a woman, all my life I had been groomed to serve as a handmaid, to speak when spoken to, to play second fiddle. I had been educated for the past, not the future. I was indistinguishable from the officers by class, by training, by upbringing. The only difference was that they were paid and I worked for free. No wonder I was ineffective. Glumly I eyed my own futility.

What to do? Resignation from the Bench would achieve nothing; they would probably be glad to see the back of me. I had tried doing good and had quite a reputation as an activist, but that cut no ice in a system in which voluntary action had no recognised place. I had worked hard at being a cog in the machinery of government. Yet to what purpose? Reluctantly I came to the conclusion that to be a voluntary worker in the welfare state was simply not enough. However sound the system of administration, the ultimate responsibility for making the decisions which would control its operation would lie elsewhere. If I was to be anything like effective in working towards my long-term goal, that was where I must be. And that meant that I would have to jump the counter and become a politician.

I found it a difficult decision to take, reared as I had been in the tradition of the moral superiority of the voluntary worker as against the statutory. I had no ambition to be a City Councillor and was suspicious of the restrictions party membership would impose on my freedom. Though I loyally accepted my obligations once I became a member, I never concealed the fact that my motive was not commitment to the Labour Party; party membership was to me a means to what I regarded as a much greater end. It was an honesty that once nearly had me thrown off the list of approved candidates because, on being asked where I would look for inspiration, I failed to give the politically correct reply. Eleanor Rathbone had triumphed as an Independent because of her personal circumstances but that option was no longer available. Either I went the whole hog and signed on the dotted line or I must retire to the fringes and forever hold my peace.

Even as I dithered, the Conservatives blundered. In 1961, after six years in power, Labour lost control and on taking over, the Tories, as was usual, allocated a ration of coopted places on the Education Committee to the minority parties. However, in a break from custom, they insisted on making the nominations for these places themselves, and chose to strike me from the list. At first, I accepted my exclusion in the true sporting tradition of my public school, gratified to hear on the grape-vine that I was regarded as a 'dangerous woman'. Then an incident occurred in the Juvenile Court that startled me out of my acquiescence. A white mother from Windsor Street appeared before us in support of her two lads who had both been in trouble before. She was a big woman, warm, real Liverpool stuff. When I asked her to tell us about her boys, she leant on the huge slab of mahogany behind which we sat so defensively. Tears ran gently down her face as she explained that she was Liverpool born and bred herself but nobody would give her boys a chance because their father was black. He had gone back to Ghana to make a home for them all and she hoped to follow quite soon if only we did not send the boys away: perhaps out there they would have the chance denied to them here.

I was profoundly ashamed. It was this mother who should be sitting in the seat of judgement, not me. It wasn't justice that we handed out in the Juvenile Court. The law was simply not relevant to boys like hers whose delinquency was rooted in a quagmire of deprivation not of their own making. Overcome by what Josephine Butler once called the 'awesome burden of compassion', I found myself driven to accept that I could no longer acquiesce. Compliance in a system of government which could produce such injustice was simply beyond my capacity to endure. Then and there I determined that somehow I must become a City Councillor.

We had joined the Labour Party some years previously, less out of any commitment to its programme than as a gesture of support for our stalwart Member of Parliament, Bessie Braddock, whose battles on behalf of students returning from the services had won our hearts. She was then under threat of deselection by an extremist element in the local party. I took to ward politics like a duck to water; it was a splendid escape from such restrictive gatherings as that of the University Ladies' Tea Club. The buccaneering atmosphere of the Abercromby Ward was a reflection of the Chicago-Boss style of the Liverpool party as a whole. Bessie's rumbustious promotion of the interests of the down-trodden rapidly became legendary. Every Friday night, she came straight from the House of Commons to meet her ward secretaries, of which I became one, and issue directives for the work of the next week. For years the ward met in what had been the front bedroom of an old house in Falkner Square owned by a branch of some Trade Union. Used as a drinking club, it was periodically raided by the police. Our affairs were master-minded by a Catholic widow, the classic matriarch of inner city life. Her web of contacts included the barmaid at the pub in town where the real politicking went on, who regaled us as we sat in Ma's kitchen with a running commentary by 'phone of the progress of whatever row was taking place.

Having thus worked my passage as ward secretary, I was duly approved by John ('Jack') Braddock for inclusion in the list of candidates. I vaguely re-member being interviewed in a romantic slum of an office in Manchester Street just by the Mersey Tunnel entrance, all cobwebbed with nostalgia for the past, its walls plastered with faded photographs of early warriors, framed Trade Union certificates of membership, weather-beaten banners. It stirred my sense of history, however much the individuals I met might fall short of my expectations. If I was disconcerted by the realities of party politics, I was in no way deterred.

In due course, I was invited to stand for the Allerton Ward, an area then greatly sought after by the aspiring respectable: such Council housing as had been built reflected the privet-hedge mentality of suburbia. The ward had accepted its lot as a thorn in the side of a compulsively conservative area and a training ground for embryo politicians such as myself, a job they took ser-iously, much to my benefit. Canvassing was a tedious business: open the gate, walk up the little path, plop literature through the letter box, walk back down the path, latch the gate and on to the next, all with never a sign of a living being other than the fierce dogs that snatched at my fingers even as I poked a leaflet through the door. Needless to add that we lost, though we did rather better than usual, I being a ladylike person, wife of a Professor and with a bit of a reputation as a magistrate and do-gooder. Allerton shook me; it was so buttoned-up, so withdrawn, so private. I made a peculiar speech at the count about being disturbed by the poverty of life as lived in Allerton, compared with that in Abercromby. They must have thought me mad, but I really meant it. Then I hastened back to Liverpool 8, vowing never again to seek fame or fortune abroad.

I was interviewed by the Granby Ward in 1962 in the bleak setting of a class-room in the old Board School. The active membership consisted of four widows and one man, average age in the seventies. The leading figure was yet another of the matriarch class, a woman whose husband had been sacked after the Police Strike of 1919 of which she talked as of a recent event. She recollected trundling a handcart along the Dock Road to provide a platform for Jimmy Sexton and others in the grand old days of the dawn of the Labour Party. Our solitary man was a compositor, with slug-like pallor and unpredict-able working hours but he was all we had. The Braddocks had instructed that I was to be selected as a candidate so I duly was.

The whole business of running the election was ramshackle in the extreme. The financing was pathetic, as I had no reliable Trade Union support. Printing poll cards was the one big unavoidable expense. It was firmly believed that you could lose an election if you failed to send out individual hand-addressed cards to every voter on the list, all sixteen thousand of them. A lot of people rallied round just for the fun of it who never attended ward meetings and were certainly not even members. Old ladies took home great piles of 'writing up', the election became a highly entertaining participant event. I recollect many a companionable evening in various 'front rooms' when six or eight of us scribbled like mad, drinking tea and swopping political gossip. Delivering the cards with so little manpower was an education in itself of the geography of the area. The compositor and I delivered the last of the poll cards at two in the morning on election day. That we should win what had previously been a Tory ward was indeed a miracle. I could only suppose that I was a visible symbol of security and respectability to a community suffering from a surfeit of disintegration.

As we crept home exhausted after the count, I cried out to my husband in amazement, 'now what have we gone and done?'!

Chapter 8
THE GLORY THAT WAS GRANBY

In which first-hand experience of life in the Granby Ward in Toxteth focuses my attention on the practicalities of community development. My commitment to the principle of universal social
responsibility is constantly refreshed by my involvement in local
affairs as an elected member.

At first sight, when my husband and I went canvassing in the run-up to the
1963 local elections, Granby looked agreeable enough, like a newly retired
gent with years of good service behind him but a period of useful life still
to come. The streets were wide and handsome, in the Liverpool merchant
tradition. Many were tree-lined, though, for lack of pruning, lights burned
all day in some houses. Victorian residences lined the major thoroughfares
which were cut across by streets of smaller houses, each a replica in miniature
of its grander neighbours. It still looked what it had originally been intended
to be when it was rushed up in 1868 and 1869: an essentially respectable neighbourhood for those whose aim in life was to lever themselves up out of the
down-town slums. True, at the Lodge Lane end, there was an intrusion of later
bye-law housing, close-packed into straight street after straight street, but
even there a code of respectability was rigidly enforced. There were more
churches to the half-mile of Princes Avenue than would accommodate the
entire population had they chosen to attend. For the sake of respectability,
no factories, workshops, or public houses were permitted.

I was under no illusion that this pleasant picture was anything more than a
facade behind which lay deep trouble. The whole area was just plain old. The
entire fabric of the environment—drains, streets, lights, houses, water
supply—had all been brought into being precisely a century ago when legislation had set this slice of King John's great Toxteth Park free at last for development. Now, for lack of maintenance, their useful life was done. At the same
time, the standards of respectable living had soared. A privy in the backyard,
however spotlessly white-washed, was no longer acceptable. Two bedrooms
were no longer tolerable for families with growing children. (I never did

manage to discover how the practicalities of living were dealt with when grown sons and daughters shared a single room and the closet was outside in the yard.) 'Clear the lot' was the fashionable response. Hence Eden Street.

Eden was one of a set of streets all called after rivers. We had canvassed Cam, Exe and Thames. Our reception had been courteous if not cordial, this being Tory territory, but lively enough. The chill silence of Eden Street came as a physical shock. No children played on the pavement here. No passers-by greeted us. Every house was sealed up with galvanised sheets as if a plague had struck. Once a street of minuscule copies of the Victorian mansions on the Boulevard, complete with lace curtains, well-scrubbed doorsteps and the strictly enforced pattern of behaviour that went with them, now it stood desolate. It had been known to us party workers as a staunch stronghold of that curious breed, the Liverpool working-class Conservative. All that had gone. Now it stood as a dumb witness to the onset of the first Clearance Order to afflict Granby. Eden Street symbolised for me what was to become the theme of all my time as a councillor. It stood for the obliteration of the way of life of a right little, tight little human society, and the dispersal of those who for a hundred years had relied on it for security and care—all gone, who knew where?

I started out bravely enough. It was in those days a point of honour for us Councillors to see for ourselves the conditions under which the people lived who came to our weekly 'surgeries'. Being a housewife with time at my own command, this presented no problem and I quickly earned a reputation for zeal. I was acutely aware of the gulf between what was expected of me and what I could hope to achieve, but I clung to my belief that for me at least, the strategy must be to focus on 'knitting up the fabric of a disintegrating society'. It was a faith that was happily confirmed when early on I was approached by a handful of tenants in one of the 'rivers' streets whose landlord demanded an unreasonable increase in their rents. I encouraged them to stand fast in unity and to their astonishment and my gratification, the landlord climbed down. The obvious next step, obvious to me at least, was for them to form a cooperative to buy up all the properties. But although my husband assembled all the necessary detail from Sweden and elsewhere, the scheme never got off the ground. The tenants were capable enough, and interested, but they lacked every single necessary resource; they had neither the know-how nor a typewriter, neither self-confidence nor a telephone. This incident renewed my enthusiasm for the campaign to persuade the City Council to accept that community development was a Good Thing for which they should accept responsibility. As a member of the Education Committee I was now in a much better position to speak for the voluntary movement with which I had been so long associated; this was precisely the reason why I had wanted to be a Councillor.

Meanwhile, the housing situation in the city generally was implacably moving towards crisis. The only remedy for the wholesale decay of an ageing environment seemed to many to be an equally wholesale programme of clearance. No wonder we fell for new estates and quick-build multi-storey blocks with all mod-cons. I struggled to argue the case against clearance and for the regeneration of what, in the days when Eleanor Rathbone had represented Granby, had been such a self-respecting community. Compared with the glamour of a house with an indoor lavatory, my prattle about traditions of neighbourliness made little headway. Then quite unexpectedly, in the year after my election, what had been a doddering decline into old age common to the inner areas, developed a turn of speed which was to endow the situation with a quality of sheer horror.

Improbably enough, this was triggered off by the publication of the Robbins *Report on Higher Education* (cmnd 2154-1, London, HMSO, 1963). Robbins plugged the case for expansion and the 1960s were consequently honeymoon years for the universities. Notably so in Liverpool, where the University was situated in the Abercromby Ward immediately next door to Granby. The University's acquisition of some eighty acres of land presented them with splendid opportunities for expansion which were grasped with commendable zeal by both town and gown.

There was however, one consequence whose ramifications had certainly not been anticipated; the clearance of the area entailed the expulsion of the closely packed mass of human beings who had found refuge there after being blitzed out of their customary homes down by the docks. As the University programme developed, more and more people found themselves under pressure to get out of what at best had only been a precarious resting place. Belatedly the Bloody Octopus (as older inhabitants still describe the University) did its best to speed them on their way. But where to? The housing shortage in the city generally was such that there was literally nowhere for them to go, except in Granby, where vast Victorian villas stood vacant and crumbling, their onetime owners long since gone, driven away by the savagery of the blitz.

Into the vacuum was sucked the medley of people uprooted from Abercromby, their bits and pieces stacked on handcarts or perambulators, their children trailing at their heels. Land sharks were quick to take over, cash mysteriously in hand, prepared to rent out their acquisitions room by room. They made no attempt to remedy the deficiencies of basic amenities beyond the provision of a shilling-in-the-slot gas cooker on each landing for shared use: it was a tribute to the amazing tolerance of the assortment of tenants that this difficult arrangement seldom resulted in open violence. A single lavatory for as many as fifteen tenancies gave rise to unimaginable squalor. Such small part of me as was able to remain detached, eyed with wry relish the contrast between the surviving splendours of Victorian domesticity and their current usage.

Crowded into rabbit warrens of multi-lets, what developed was not unlike a transit camp for refugees. Refugees they certainly were. Through no fault of their own, they were homeless and rootless and as such, unwanted and rejected. Moreover, their faces were frequently black.

There had for some time been a corner of the ward which was known to us as the Black Square, for self-evident reasons, but it had been possible to ignore its existence because it was separated from the rest of the neighbourhood by the wide sweep of the Princes Avenue boulevard. This delusion of harmony was disturbed by the arrival of the incomers from Abercromby. As the pressure on accommodation in the big multi-lets grew, inevitably the overflow seeped into the side streets. This created a very different situation. Our MP, Bessie Braddock, boasted that there was no racial prejudice in Liverpool, a boast which had never been challenged because the 'coloured', being largely seamen, accepted that their proper place was down by the docks and stayed in it. Now they were spilling over into what was not their 'proper place'. For some time the tradition of keeping up appearances held good. The refugees from Abercromby were eyed with a shocked surprise which reminded me of the reaction with which our suburb had greeted the evacuees from Liverpool. Only in the privacy of our housing surgeries did white families seeking to be rehoused reveal as their real reason the fact that 'the blacks have moved into our street'.

So, to our considerable astonishment we, as councillors, found ourselves called on to represent two entirely different groups of people, whose interests on occasion were in direct conflict. The stoicism with which both old inhabitants and new incomers bore their enforced co-existence constantly amazed me, as did the fortitude with which they tolerated conditions that I would have found intolerable. The entire make-up of the original community was drastically changed. There were disproportionately high numbers of the young and of the old. The number of those of parent age who might be relied on to maintain social discipline and take care of the sick and old were patently inadequate to take the strain. Granby became a haven—or a dumping ground—for the unwanted of society. No normal provision for welfare, no amount of caring by the community could begin to carry that load.

This was no static situation. Flux and change was the order of the day.

Clearance, grasping landlords, mounting unemployment, the ebb and flow of the rootless and home-less, each fed the other as the pace quickened. The skids were under our feet. A once stable community was disintegrating before our very eyes. Helpless in the face of the avalanche of pleas for help which descended on us at our 'surgeries', all we could do was offer to bring the relevant officials to meet local residents on their home ground. But who in that disorganised medley of people was to find premises for a meeting, get round the streets with circulars advertising the time and place, make sure that the relevant officers attended, and organise the follow-up after the meeting? Salvation, though at first I failed to recognise it as such, came from an un-expected source. Scandalised by the housing conditions endured by members of their highly respectable congregations, a handful of Granby clergy of all three denominations had come together for mutual support. Inevitably, with-out deliberate intent, they found themselves with no choice but to become involved in a whole range of local issues that were highly political. At which point, of course, our paths began to cross.

Inspired by Keir Murren, pastor of a near-by Domestic Mission who cher-ished a vision of what could be achieved by cooperation on a community basis, our Granby clergy had bravely formed themselves into what became known as the Neighbourhood Group of Churches. This in the context of the rabid sectarianism of Liverpool tradition was as near a miracle as could be hoped for.

Not for nothing was the lead taken by Donald May, the minister at the Methodist Church in Princes Avenue (see D. May and M. Simey, *The Servant Church in Granby*, Liverpool, Centre for Urban Studies, University of Liverpool, 1989). Reared in the Methodist tradition of involving even the humblest of its members in practical service, May's vision of the Servant Church as the pur-pose of a church's existence in the inner city provided a sound foundation for a policy of community development. The churches of all three denominations put their entire resources at our disposal. They lent their premises to street groups without regard to whether they were churchgoers or not. They under-took secretarial work, drafted letters to officials, allowed us to use their tele-phones, provided transport to take groups to public hearings and meetings. Church members certainly contributed an invaluable element of experience as organisers. Most important of all, the churches' participation injected into all that we did a constant reminder of the moral implications of our activities for the community of which we were members. Donald May taught us more about social morality through discussions at committee meetings than by his sermons.

How far their respective congregations approved of what ensued I very much doubt. What was evident was that without them, our attempts to galvanise the residents into some kind of united action would have got nowhere. I was mortified to find that the Labour Party could never attract an audience to a street meeting, whereas, with the backing of the churches, we were assured of a full house. Not only residents but the many people who worked in the neighbourhood were clearly reassured by the sponsorship of the clergy, an invaluable asset, incidentally, for me as a Labour Councillor in what had previously been a Tory ward.

Though there was much talk about community development and even, in academic circles, of 'consumer sovereignty', there was a wildly confusing lack of precision as to what it was all about. It was left to the planners to bring us down to earth, quite literally. There on the maps which they displayed at our residents' meetings, all carefully defined down to the last lamp-post, were the streets designated for clearance. The planners were amongst the first to grasp that clearance and housing schemes must involve public participation if they were to prove acceptable to those involved. They were assiduous in their attendance at meetings and in their wake came all manner of representatives of relevant services right across the board of environmental improvement. The contribution made by these officers was often done voluntarily in their own time. It received little commendation other than from residents who had never before been treated as partners in government. Though their reception was sometimes rough, both sides profited, local people in their grasp of the conduct of public affairs and the officers from first hand introduction to the people on the receiving end of their proposals.

The prospect of clearance proved to be the universal experience which drew people together in a way that was a revelation to us all. At first, everyone was hungry for information as to what their own fate would be and desperate for assurance that they were in the right queue for the overspill estate of their choice. Having access as a Councillor to all the Corporation departments, I came into my own. Full of energy and delighted to be of use, I scurried between the Ward, Council committee meetings and the offices of the various Departments, constituting a two-way liaison service which won me a response locally which I found infinitely gratifying. My 'surgeries' developed into a support service. There was nothing I could do to influence anyone's chances of being rehoused but apparently the sincerity of my respect for the way in which women in particular dealt with their burden of care was so rare an experience as to be worth coming to see me—just for that reason. I never ceased to feel deeply humbled by the contrast between their lives of heroism and my own prim existence as a University wife. Could this be really me, I cried out in amazement, like the old woman in the nursery tale who woke from a roadside nap to find her skirts had been sheared off at the knee by some prankster.

Imperceptibly, the cold fact began to emerge that clearance was likely to be a long drawn-out process—if indeed it ever happened—and that hope of being rehoused was a day-dream for all except the most sorely afflicted. Residents' meetings ceased to focus on the decorative street maps of the planners. Instead the little men in bowler hats, as the cartoons had it, representing the public health services, found themselves the target for an avalanche of demands for help in making the best of a situation that was evidently to be with us for some time to come. How to force landlords to do basic repairs; how to get the bins emptied; how to improve the water supply and have the drains cleared—this last the issue of which the Liberals made such profitable use at election times. It quickly became apparent to those who suffered such conditions at first hand that their only hope lay in getting together to voice their common concerns. Individuals learned by experience that they were liable to be shouted down if they tried to air their personal woes at meetings.

Those who had never wanted to move out in the first place began to take fresh heart. Maybe there was an alternative to clearance after all? There was even talk of 'our community'. Older inhabitants gathered up courage to defend the values of the way of life to which they had long been accustomed. It was obvious that if the head of steam generated by the argument over whether to stay or not was to be put to good use, support and resources would have to be put at the disposal of the residents. I had pestered on about the need for an official community development service as a local authority responsibility ever since we had come back from the West Indies. By good fortune, this particular pot came to the boil just when Granby was ready to benefit from such a service and, in 1965, one of the first Community Development Officers was appointed by the Corporation.

Phil Doran was a highly professional and experienced community worker, self-disciplined and un-bossy. He saw his rôle as being to work with and for people, with a view to enabling them to tap such resources as were available and to carry their responsibilities as citizens effectively. He was equally clear that, unlike the clergy, what people then decided to do was none of his business as a Council employee. This interpretation was later to be challenged by politicians who insisted that a community worker ought to forward the policies of the party in power, an argument that rumbles on to this day and subsequently led to some fine old conflicts. Slowly, something like order began to emerge out of this plethora of activity. Sheer pressure of need effectively turned the Church Group into a general community resource and this provided the basis for the formation in 1967 of the Granby Community Council.

The Community Council consisted of representatives of as many streets as chose to take up the opportunity, together with sundry coopted members such as myself. Its purpose was to help local people to join together to tackle their common problems and to enable them to present a united front in dealing with officialdom. The Chair was habitually taken by one or other of the three clergymen, although critics carped at the leading part they played in its affairs. This might perhaps have been justified had this been a stable community but it was certainly not merited in the context of the wholesale disintegration from which Granby was suffering. The churches were the only fixed point in a world of uncertainty; researchers commented that even the children at Granby Street school changed their addresses with dizzy frequency.

What it was that distinguished the contribution of church workers from that of the official youth and community workers eluded me at the time. It was only after the disturbances of 1981 that I began to understand that what characterised our particular little group was that they were, quite simply, on our side. They were there to serve us, not the establishment. Officials could and did tell us how to operate the machinery of government; the churches stood alongside us on our metaphorical barricades. I found it deeply moving to experience at first hand that injection of morality into politics such as had been the driving force behind the early Labour movement in Liverpool.

Once they began to meet together, residents were quick to draw their own conclusions as to the root causes of the malaise that afflicted their once-respected neighbourhood. They might be ill-informed but they were no fools and it was obvious to them that equality of provision in principle did not necessarily result in equality in practice. A flat rate of grant aid that ignored the special needs of the inner areas, whether directed to the emptying of our bins or the teaching of our children, struck us as plain nonsense, especially after Bishop Sheppard produced figures showing that Granby paid more in rates than it received in services. Demands for attention to 'me and my leaky roof' began to give way to a sharper note of protest. 'It's not fair' became the common cry. Education provided a classic example.

Granby Street Board School had been built in 1869 to meet the needs of the rapidly developing new estate. It was a great barracks of a building of the kind so rightly admired by Charles Booth when they were built, with big light rooms, high ceilings, stark stone staircases and outside lavatories which froze in the winter. In its day, or rather in Granby's great days, it had had a proud record of academic success, all duly enshrined in letters of gilt on the Honours Boards. That day was long since past. The premises were no longer adequate by the educational standards of the twentieth century: there were too many children and too few facilities. Most disturbingly, the traditional code of social discipline on which school life depended had been undermined by the disintegration of the community which had originally imposed it. Teachers who chose to work there were regarded as committing professional suicide. The staff turnover was as rapid as that of the children themselves, and there were often spells when no replacement could be found. It was apparent to parents and Managers alike that a flat rate of education provision for the city as a whole spelled nothing less than a totally unjustifiable inequality for schools such as ours.

Appointment as a School Manager was a political perk—it looked good on an election manifesto—but we contrived the selection of the wife of a local Councillor and then proceeded to make her Chairman in place of an aged incumbent who had blocked all progress for years. She proved to be a bonny fighter—her major asset, in addition to considerable personal charm, being a total lack of experience of committee work which enabled her to press merrily ahead regardless of custom and habit.

Out of meetings with the chairmen and heads of neighbouring schools and with parents, a Granby Action Group evolved, which in turn, was a prototype for the National Association of Governors and Managers, fondly known as NAG'M. The Education Committee was eventually persuaded to accept responsibility for a city-wide programme of training and information for school governors. Teaching in schools like Granby Street acquired a glamour that infused the education system with an enthusiasm and crusading zeal such as had previously been sadly lacking. Advisers actually began to recommend teachers for promotion on the grounds that they had had experience in an inner area. When the Plowden Report on *Children and their Primary Schools* (London, HMSO, 1967) actually recommended the designation of Education Priority Areas, local people remarked with gratification that Plowden had obviously listened to what they had to say. The outcome was the setting up in the inner area of what was called the Priority Project. This demonstrated with remarkable success that parents did in fact care about the education of their children and could be actively involved in the process.

Certainly there was material galore for the Community Council to get to grips with: street lighting, the bare-faced dumping of unwanted furniture and builders' rubbish, and the endless uncertainties of clearance. Of the many issues we pursued, perhaps the most gratifying was the long-drawn out campaign to rid the neighbourhood of its reputation as a red light area—could it be that our success was due to the fact that for once no official body claimed it as their territory from which the likes of us must be excluded?

The Street Offences Act of 1959 was designed to clear prostitution off the pavements of streets like Lime Street where it was practised openly in the bright lights of the city centre. The outcome for Granby was disastrous. The clubs run in the big houses along Princes Avenue by various Afro-Caribbean communities for their own nationals found themselves swamped by an alien influx. By the mid-1960s the situation was right out of control. No woman, however old or ill-favoured, could walk the streets with impunity. With my white hair, I myself was accosted, presumably on the assumption that I must be a madam. Little girls were trailed on their way to school even though accompanied by their mothers, with a frequency whose significance is only now generally realised. Back entries and front doorsteps (including our own because we had a pillared porch) were littered with contraceptives which the children seized on for balloons.

Ironically, matters were brought to a head when in 1967, on the opening of the newly re-built Methodist church and community centre, the low wall surrounding the premises was taken over by young women, many from outside the area, waiting to attract the attention of kerb crawlers. Neither church nor residents could stand for that and the offence to public morality inspired a determined response. Discovering that the law was no help to us, we patrolled the streets ourselves taking down car numbers to be passed to the police for discreet attention. Learning to our astonishment that permission given twenty years ago for a scout troop to use the ground floor of a house on the boulevard still held good for a bunch of outsiders to run a night-club, we doggedly opposed every attempt to open clubs and secure licences.

My happiest recollection of many is that of a trojan couple who dated back to the pioneering days of the Labour party and who lived opposite a particularly obnoxious club. Led by them, the residents banded together, hired a lawyer, raised his fee by jumble sales, and set out for court in a minibus to oppose the granting of a licence. After the first few had given evidence, the Chairman of the Bench indicated that enough was enough. But the troops had waited months for this hour and they insisted that each must say their piece. There was something like twenty of them. No Bench could resist such an assembly of righteous indignation. We won. We subsequently heard that the word had gone round amongst club owners that it was no use trying to open premises in Granby because of the opposition that would be encountered.

It is tempting to fall into the trap of endlessly reminiscing about those oddly happy years. On the one hand such misery, such squalor, such utter waste of human lives. Yet on the other, the quite stunning commitment to the basic values of human existence. We let down our buckets wherever and whenever opportunity occurred, like the captain of the ship becalmed offshore and in desperate need of fresh water. The outcome was that individuals began to sense that they were by no means the hapless nonentities they had assumed themselves to be.

And there was, too, the growing excitement as we discovered anew the significance of the old adage that united we could stand. What we came up with was a recipe for the development of an urban community. The basis was a profound respect for the individual and a refusal to accept the denial of dignity handed out to us as a community by 'government' such as the police. Put into practice, that called for know-how and information and that in turn gave us an appetite for opportunities for action. It was the lesson of the West Indies all over again. Democracy must be based on access to the rights and duties of membership of the community, not as a privilege but as of right. In so doing, Granby became a demonstration plot for the regeneration of a disintegrated community. As our resident 'detached priest' put it:

> The inner City of Liverpool was alive with community work. I remain indebted to that era and the friends I made; I came across dedication and commitment, not to mention love, in the lives of full-time and part-time community workers. For me it was an experience of the signs of the Kingdom of God at work in many lives not even knowledgeable about, never committed to, that Kingdom. (Austin Smith, *Journeying with God*, London, Sheed & Ward, 1990, p. 129)

We all of us felt that we were pioneers. Though we were duly humbled by the magnitude of the forces that worked against us, that was countered—certainly on my part—by my unshakable conviction that the way ahead lay in patiently plodding towards the creation of a society in which every member had a right to a share in the management of our common affairs. Given that, I was confident that the machinery of government could surely be made to work. Reform and regeneration were what was required, not revolution. We eyed with hostility a plague of amateur anarchists in dirty white plimsolls who descended on us, happy to live on their dole, hell-bent on rousing us to revolt.

Our big chance came when in 1969 there was a change in national housing policy from wholesale clearance to a programme for the general rehabilitation of the inner areas. Shelter, the national charity concerned with the homeless, was then on the crest of a wave of public support following the TV film *Cathy Come Home*. Taking advantage of this, they decided to extend their scope from individual need to a scheme that would involve both public and private resources in a comprehensive programme for the regeneration of an entire neighbourhood.

No sooner said than done. For a variety of reasons, not least because the existence of the Community Council was evidence that local cooperation was likely to be secured, a small area of the Ward was selected, henceforth to be known as the Granby Triangle. Full of enthusiasm, the Shelter Neighbourhood Action Group (SNAP) took over (see *SNAP 69/72*, sponsored by Shelter, 1972). I found myself tossed up on a bank and left there high and dry while the tide swept past me. A Steering Committee sprang up from nowhere, headed by the traditional Liverpool business philanthropist. I wangled myself on to it by dint of asking such awkward questions at the City Council to which no one knew the answers, that the only way to silence me was to appoint me as a Council representative. The Community Council was allocated a couple of places and there was, of course, a powerful contingent from Shelter. Premises were found in a decayed villa which had previously housed a police station and a high-powered Director appointed who had relevant experience in Ulster. I doubt if at that stage there was much understanding or enthusiasm on the part of most of the SNAP committee for the principle of resident participation. However, top priority was, we were assured, to be given to the needs and wishes of the local people and to this end, Task Forces of residents were set up to identify specific shortcomings and devise remedies. Experts were called in at Shelter's expense to act as a 'civil service of the streets' to advise these groups as to possible solutions and prepare the case for presentation to those in authority.

No one commented on the absence of black faces from our meetings. The majority of the locally-born blacks were still youngsters and their difficulties were seen as part and parcel of the 'juvenile problem' in general. In any case, the Triangle was occupied almost entirely by long-established white families so how could it be otherwise?

After all sorts of hurly-burly concerning such bureaucratic obstacles as securing recognition as a General Improvement Area, progress began to become apparent. Overnight, by private negotiation between unspecified locals and workers on a nearby site, a large wooden hut appeared in the garden of SNAP's premises to serve as a community resource. This boosted the morale of the Community Council which had previously lacked any kind of meeting place of its own.

What fun we had. What an exhilarating experience it was to argue and to plan and then to see our recommendations actually carried out before our very eyes. Applications for improvement grants shot up in the most satisfactory manner. Space was ingeniously devised in two-down-and-two-ups for bathrooms and indoor lavatories. Back entries were widened to make for better bin emptying. Roads were blocked off to discourage kerb crawlers and divert the twice-daily menace of commuter traffic to and from the suburbs. The crusading zeal of the SNAP team carried all gloriously forward to the great day in 1970 when the splendidly imaginative vision of Granby New Town was launched with all the hoo-ha the media could provide.

Yet for all the momentum generated by the Project and the undeniable victories scored over the entanglements of red tape, progress remained disappointingly erratic. Gradually SNAP's focus narrowed down to an increasingly ferocious attack on local government as practised in Liverpool. Our Task Forces had demonstrated the potential of a comprehensive and coordinated programme of environmental improvement; it was the failure of the establishment to respond that was the obstacle to progress. As SNAP became ever more heavily locked into battle with 'the system', its protestations of respect for local people became ever more suspect. I was myself told bluntly that they had picked me over for what I was worth and had no further use for me; there was no place for the likes of me as an elected member in their scheme of things. To residents, SNAP, in turn, became 'Them', patrons and champions perhaps, but no longer our servants. They fought for us, not with us.

Significantly, the relationship between SNAP and the Community Council was never a wholly comfortable one, though Council members constituted the backbone of the Task Forces. The SNAP team were, by their own admission, young, impatient and arrogant, characteristics which, faced with the established cohorts of the establishment, they themselves regarded as major assets. Members of the Community Council were less certain, for all that they appreciated the environmental improvements and the hope of a better future which these inspired. Local people were offended by being used as material for national fund-raising and responded to a muck-raking press with an indignant rebuttal of Shelter's advertising of their woes: deprived they certainly were, but not poor in the derogatory sense implied by the media.

Again, local residents found it hard to share SNAP's enthusiasm for 'grass roots' types who, it was claimed, knew more about crime because they had been to prison, the 'university of life', than respectable people would ever learn. SNAP, for its part, found it hard to appreciate the priority the Community Council gave to the fight against kerb crawling. Its proud boast that its vast case-load covered people from far and near and comprised need of an unimaginable variety, struck those of us who were then labouring to implement the Seebohm Report (op. cit.) on the organisation of the social services as crass folly. What it all boiled down to was that SNAP's target was the reform of the system of government, whereas the Community Council stood for the promotion of a code of values. At one unforgettable public meeting in the Methodist Centre, a brave man stood up to protest that no number of bathrooms or benefits would improve the quality of life unless public morality was given top priority.

When in 1972 the Project came to its end, SNAP faded away leaving little wrack behind so far as resident responsibility for local government was concerned. Gently the waters closed over our heads. Shelter packed its bags and left for pastures new. SNAP's gallant Director galloped away to break a lance—and perhaps his heart—against those in control in high places. Even the hut vanished as mysteriously as it had come, magically transported at dead of night to a nearby children's playground run by an ex-docker. The Housing Aid Centre set up by the Corporation was our only legacy but this was a mere mock-up of the multi-service point-of-contact with the neighbourhood of our ambitions. The Community Council struggled gamely to secure the appointment of an Advisory Committee for the Centre which would give local people some say in the conduct of its affairs, but its pleas met with no response; it was allowed the use of one of the attics.

The invaluable lessons the Project, and indeed, the whole Granby experience could have taught us have never been learned, above all the fundamental importance of the basic principle that in a democracy, ultimate responsibility must remain with the governed and not the government. Granby demonstrated that 'it can be done'. SNAP's records spell out the practical implications of implementing this principle in practice: the need for a new relationship between people and government, the vital importance of skilled servicing of the community, the replacement of control by a specialist bureaucracy with a system based on the accountability of the executive to the people.

To this day, all manner of well-intentioned persons flock to the rescue of the inner areas, ignoring all that has gone before, repeating all the mistakes we made, re-inventing the wheel at our expense. The SNAP report moulders on library shelves, a topic for sad nostalgia on the part of those who once participated in that gallant attempt to achieve the redemption of their own community. The pity, the infinite pity of it. How can this have come about?

Chapter 9
THE DISINHERITED SOCIETY

In which the application of business management to local government fails to resolve the deepening crisis in the inner cities and
facilitates the takeover of the administration of community affairs
by the bureaucracy. This resulted in the extrusion of the elected
representative and the deprivation of the right of the individual
to social responsibility. Granby becomes a disinherited society.

SNAP was right, of course; there was certainly an urgent need for an overhaul
of the machinery of government. But I refused to accept their wholesale condemnation of local government and all its works which seemed to me unjustifiable. Instead I clung to my belief that 'the system' could be made to work if
we gave our minds to it. To me, that meant two things. First, that a social
policy designed to 'knit up the torn fabric of the community', as I myself
put it, by bringing neighbour together with neighbour was essential; experience in Granby had demonstrated this to be both practicable and rewarding.
Second, what SNAP had brought sharply home to us was that this alone was
not enough. There must be a warp as well as a weft if the cloth was to hold;
those who administered public services must be brought into a new and closer
relationship with those whose needs they existed to serve. At the same time,
the isolation of services—each focused on a particular specialism—must give
way to a coordinated approach which would be more directly geared to the
overall needs of the human beings for whom they were provided.

The death of my husband in 1969, and that of my old mother some time
before, set me free to commit myself wholeheartedly to the pursuit of this
dual purpose. I use the phrase deliberately. For though the ending of that
richly-rewarding companionship made heavy demands on my personal fortitude, I was abashed to discover what a practical difference it made to my
whole way of life as a politician. No longer was I burdened with guilt if I
chose to sit out a tedious committee in order to prevent some smart alec
from taking advantage of my absence to wreck a particular project of my
own. No longer did I have to refuse opportunities to hold office or to attend

conferences because I was not prepared to put politics before family. With politics legitimately my top priority, it was only then that I began to make anything like an effective contribution. I eyed my women colleagues with pity, knowing what a double burden they carried. I even began to wonder if the women's movement had lost its way. Was equality on these terms really worth pursuing? Even more disturbing, was marriage as I had known it any longer viable?

Long before I ever became a councillor, I had beavered away at devising ways and means of bringing government and governed closer together. Some progress had been made. A bold venture in shared responsibility was initiated by the Director of the City Council's Environmental Services Department under which local officers were appointed to work with community groups on such running sores as the dumping of old sofas in back entries and the off-loading of builders' rubbish. The magic lay in the fact that each officer had cash in the hand which he and the group might dispose of as they thought fit. Moreover, should other departments prove obstructive, he had instant access to the Director.

Another experiment set up following on the Plowden inquiry into primary education (op. cit.), went under the title of Priority. Priority set out to demonstrate that inner city parents did care about the education of their children, given the opportunity. The opportunity as envisaged by Priority took the form of a partnership between teachers and parents that produced results beyond the belief of those who remembered the days of locked playground gates and notices saying 'Parents Keep Out' see Eric Midwinter, *Priority Education*, Harmondsworth, Penguin, 1972).

That in turn led to the creation in 1968 of the Pre-school Organisations' Committee (POC). Provision for children under school age was an interest dear to my heart, not least because of my memories of the difficulties I had encountered in rearing an only child. Pre-school provision sat uneasily as a responsibility of both the Education and Social Services Departments. As I served on both committees, I was nicely placed to push for coordination, not only between the different services involved but between the statutory bodies and the voluntary workers who were responsible for most of the play groups.

What developed was a truly remarkable piece of machinery for the coordination of statutory responsibility with voluntary activity. POC was made up of representatives from the voluntary groups, together with councillors from the two departments involved. Serviced by City Council officials from both Social Services and the City Treasury, POC met on Corporation premises and was to all intents and purposes a sub-committee of Social Services, with the vital difference that it nevertheless preserved its total autonomy. The preparation of the pre-school section of the Annual Budget and the allocation of grants were undertaken by POC and presented to Social Services for ratification. So well-informed were the members as to each other's activities that applications were submitted to a devastating scrutiny which consequently won considerable credibility. The secret of POC's success was undoubtedly the cross-fertilisation of the expertise of the advisers and administrators with the first-hand experience of the grass-roots voluntary workers, each preserving their own autonomy.

Much more difficult was the struggle to break down the barriers between the different professions. I became involved in the drive to prise the Social Services out of the control of the medical profession and set them up on their own. Eventually, in 1968 the long-awaited Seebohm Report (op. cit.) brought official support for the creation of a separate Social Services Department and we embarked on all the fun of building a new empire and setting up a new Committee. Our emancipation from medical control was, however, only partial; the Deputy Medical Officer of Health having now become redundant was appointed as Director of Social Services. I was approached as to whether I intended to lay claim to the Chairmanship but in true womanly tradition, I was content to accept the post of Deputy, the Chair going to Cyril Taylor, a Toxteth Councillor who was also a doctor, though fortunately an enthusiast for community development.

Our policy was directed to democratising the service, though I don't think that was how we put it at the time. We held staff meetings with gatherings of lesser social workers and administrative staff. For many to meet the committee face-to-face was a startling innovation which literally left them dumbfounded. We coopted voluntary workers on to the main Committee where to our disappointment they meekly accepted the rôle of advisers, speaking only when spoken to. The provision of Home Helps and Good Neighbours was a priority. Partnership was our key word. We were peculiarly fortunate in that our deputy chief officer was not only a man of experience as a Relieving Officer under the Poor Law, but also a Methodist lay preacher whose principles infused our activities with a welcome element of political morality.

Nevertheless, with an increasingly heavy heart, I had to admit that such successes as we achieved were exceptions to the general rule. By and large, the wheels of government ground ever more slowly and with greater inadequacy. Do-As-You-Did-Before was our only policy, I remember crying bitterly during a debate on the Education budget. The whole system was in danger of seizing up. Indeed the reorganisation of local government nationally was, at that time, the subject of endless inquiry and debate. While that argument dragged on, the City Council resolved to set its own house in order. Thus it was that in 1969 there walked on to our stage a most astonishing apparition in the shape of Corporate Man.

McKinsey's team of business management experts were, I suppose the first of the new breed now known as 'yuppies'. Excessively 'London', expensively tailored with the most beautiful collection of ties and manners to match, they tried to call me Margaret which I, being far behind the times, regarded as impertinence. I remember one session where they mystified us by repeatedly referring to someone called Charles, by whom it emerged they meant the Director of Education whose first name we had never before heard used. They invited me out to expensive lunches which I refused, to their visible incomprehension. They knew nothing of local government and went on to greater glory elsewhere on the strength of what we taught them, but they never learned that money isn't the only thing that makes people tick. Poor Mr Bland-the-Baths, for example: as an ex-naval type, the shining pipes and steaming boilers of the baths and washhouses were the joy of his life. McKinsey streamlined him out of existence and in response to our protests, assured us that they had provided a better job for him at a higher salary elsewhere in the City Council. End of conversation.

The Tories were in power then and we as a lively opposition had a whale of a time. Council meetings frequently dragged on until two in the morning. This was good rumbustious stuff in the customary style of Liverpool politics, but I was deeply uneasy. We all agreed that our affairs were in a state of right confusion, but I feared that we were in danger of falling for the dogma of the day that better management would provide the answer to all our problems. For that reason McKinsey's brief covered the activities of the administration and blandly excluded those of the elected members. As for the purpose of it all, we were back at the old game of providing for 'the poor' what we thought was good for them, or what we were prepared to pay for. There was no room for intervention by a lay public in business management except as 'customers'. Nor even perhaps for their elected representatives?

After McKinsey's departure, I watched the visible improvement in the way of working of City Council staff with all the wistfulness of a Bisto kid. The better their performance, the more conscious I became of my own inadequacy. I still typed my letters with two fingers on a typewriter that doubled as a toy for visiting grand-children. My filing system was rudimentary, mere dumps of paper in discarded shirt boxes. My constituents assumed that I was endowed with magic powers merely because I had won an election but their faith in me was often the only prop I had when I was confronted by these high-powered administrators. The forbearance with which the officers tolerated our not inconsiderable follies as elected members didn't conceal from either them or us that they could perform much more efficiently if they were given a free hand to get on with the job. 'Take us out to the Mersey Bar and drown the lot of us and no one would notice that we had gone except to welcome our departure', I exclaimed.

For all that we ran so fast and worked so hard and in spite of all our high hopes and undoubted achievements, the gulf between the needs of Granby and the provision made to meet them remained obstinately unbridgeable. Though those were times of comparative affluence, we never seemed to catch up with the galloping inflation of social stress. As fast as we identified one need and set about devising means of meeting it, yet another source of deprivation was uncovered. Gradually the area earned a name of ill-repute. *No One From L8 Need Apply* was the title of a report on youth unemployment. And equally slowly, it began to dawn on us that what we were up against in Granby was something quite new in our experience and far more sinister than anything we had ever imagined.

Our apprehension was shared by the planners. A report by Jim Amos, the City Planner, on the distribution of *Social Malaise in Liverpool* (Liverpool, Liverpool City Council, 1967), supported the protest of the outer estates that they suffered from a higher degree of specific deficiencies than the inner areas. Nevertheless, it also made crystal clear that the difficulties of life in Granby arose out of no single cause but from the multiplicity of the problems imposed on its people. It was the cumulative and on-going effect as each factor reacted on the other that was the cause of the quite exceptional level of stress which engulfed the whole neighbourhood. What my academic colleagues called the cycle of deprivation was a daily reality to local residents and one from which there could be no escape. The treadmill of despair would have been a more apt description. It seemed as if the interlock of social and economic factors had set in motion a downward spiral which it was beyond our capacity to halt, let alone reverse. This was a problem for which there was no known remedy, no resources allocated. As I put it in a City Council debate, Granby had only one industry and that a singularly flourishing one, the manufacture of social problems.

We councillors needed no reports to alert us to the consequences for the people we were supposed to represent. As clearance began to bite at the heart of the community, our housing 'surgeries' attracted longer and longer queues. Appeals for help were no longer straightforward applications for better accommodation but were expressive of a profoundly-felt resentment against the injustice of the condemnation of the entire community to a way of life against which they felt utterly helpless to protest. Though I was deeply moved by compassion for their plight, what really goaded me into activity was the passion of my respect for their capacity to survive in circumstances that I knew I myself could never cope with. The standards of decency, the triumph over squalor, which I encountered time and again left me mortified and abashed. All I could do for those who called on me for help was to give them a profoundly respectful hearing. Even that was so rare in their experience, that as one woman explained to me, they came to see me once a week simply to enjoy a few moments of my attention. The sole redeeming feature of that desperate era was, as an unusually discerning journalist remarked with incredulous disbelief, the all pervasive atmosphere of love (see Audrey Harvey, *Tenants in Danger*, Harmondsworth, Penguin, 1964). In spite of all their troubles—or perhaps because of the weight of the burden it carried?— this was a caring community.

To attribute the troubles of such determined survivors to the inadequacies or misfortunes of individuals seemed to me to be an injustice of the highest order. Given the circumstances, it simply was not possible for Granby to achieve anything approaching a civilised way of life as a community. On the contrary, it was apparent that the machinery of all that went to ensure an ordered way of living was breaking down under the strain of the exceptional overload. The irrelevance of government to the reality of existence became a fact of life. Hostility against all those in authority for their failure to deal effectively with the situation extended to the councillors. 'You're not much use, are you?' I was told by a forthright constituent. Increasing demands for the police to assert their powers of control on the streets only added to the sense of alienation: Granby was habitually referred to by them as a criminal community and policed as such. For many it was then that the seeds of resentment were sown which were to bear such bitter fruit a decade later in 1981.

The sense of stress was heightened by the fact that, nationally, the consequences of immigration from the Commonwealth had become the subject of fierce disagreement. Opinion was generally in favour of concentrating on the integration of ethnic minorities into the host community. This we prided ourselves was already being done in Liverpool 8 and, anyhow, the numbers of migrants coming to Granby were comparatively small, presumably because the prospects for housing or employment were so poor. The Methodists laid on a conference on how best to welcome people from overseas into their congregations but that apart, and despite the mounting tension between young people and the police, it was thought best to treat race as simply one factor amongst the many which compounded the situation in Granby. The significance of the fact that the majority of 'coloured' in our area were locally born Liverpudlians and not immigrants escaped attention.

That being so, I forsaw what the reaction of the Youth and Community Sub-committee would be when, in 1968, we were asked to consider the Hunt report on *Immigrants and the Youth Service* (Report of a Committee of the YSDC, London, HMSO, 1967). They would surely leave it to the officials to think up some bland response to the effect that we had few immigrants in Liverpool and no racial prejudice. My proposal that we off-load the report onto the YOC was welcomed with relief. The YOC in turn set up a working party of which both the Methodist minister from Granby and I were members, though no spokesman on behalf of the influx of black residents from Abercromby had yet emerged.

The Working Party started out cheerfully enough, expecting to do no more than report on how to maintain and improve the harmonious relations which were assumed to exist already. Some of our suburban members did not even know the whereabouts of the area we were talking about and I was hard put to it to conceal my impatience as we struggled to educate them as to the real'cies of life in the inner city. However, I must admit that we were all surprised to find that it was impossible to lay hands on any hard facts about the young and 'coloured'. Nobody knew for certain anything about this section of our community.

Those of our members who had no first-hand knowledge of the inner areas found it hard to accept that such evidence as we eventually assembled contradicted the habitual assumption that Liverpool was free from prejudice. Anecdotes about white lads being offered a job after black applicants were told that the vacancy had been filled could perhaps be discounted, but there was no denying what we could each see for ourselves, that no black faces were to be seen behind the counters of the shops in the city centre, and few black customers. A mini-survey of local industrial concerns produced a like result. We had identified a community in our midst whose existence we had never before noticed. Liverpool born and bred, surely they were entitled to a fair share of the rights of citizenship?

The title we chose put our feelings in a nutshell; the children of mixed marriages must be regarded as *Special But Not Separate* (Liverpool, Liverpool Youth Organisations Committee, 1968). The report concluded with a set of recommendations to that end, each addressed to a specific source for action. It is significant of the mystique surrounding policing that we made almost no reference to the police, in spite of the bitter resentment against their use of 'sus', the hated power to stop-and-search on suspicion.

The report was merely formally noted by the Education Committee but the effect of that was electrical. Everybody wanted to see what it was that the Committee had in effect, rejected. We sold out and had to reprint. The difficulties we had had in persuading members of the working party that prejudice did indeed exist were as nothing to the sense of outrage which our report provoked in the public at large. There was angry resentment of the very suggestion of the existence of prejudice. We were accused of provoking division in a hitherto united community. I was warned that I would split the local Labour Party if I forced the issue. I suffered a broken window or two and my re-election as a councillor was a narrow squeak because of my reputation as a partisan of the black community. I am always vulnerable to shouting in a loud voice and cowered back with a timidity of which I am to this day profoundly ashamed.

The passionate emotion which greeted what now reads as an innocuous little document is only explicable in view of the fact that its appearance had been preceded a few months earlier by Enoch Powell's notorious 'rivers of blood' speech in 1968. Setting out on my housing visits the morning after that outburst, I was immediately aware of the shiver of excited apprehension which his speech had provoked. 'Had I heard ..?' I was asked tentatively. But the question that hung unspoken in the air was '... now what? Where do we go from here?' The spectre of racial prejudice had lurked at the back of people's minds for long enough. Previously only discussed behind closed doors, now it stalked openly about our streets. What next?

Answer came there none. Locally, Donald May bravely commissioned a sculpture by Arthur Dooley, a local artist, to hang on the outside wall of the newly-built Methodist Church, which portrayed in brutal terms the suffering of a multi-racial Christ. Even as it was unveiled by the Chairman of the Methodist District, his wife was subjected to abusive phone calls. A decanting scheme to rehouse residents from the Lodge Lane area to the adjoining Kimberley estate was doggedly rejected because even though totally rebuilt, it was seen as black territory.

I myself became deeply involved in the on-going saga of the creation of a Community Relations Council whose brief would be to draw together all the various minority groups. Those were the days when we still dreamt of One World. Easier said than done. All our talk of integration seemed to be in flat contradiction of the fierce loyalty of each group to its own kind, its own culture, its own traditions. Some took to running clubs for their own members whose open doors attracted undesirable customers and the attention of the police. Others secured official grants in aid of conventional community centres, stoutly refusing any suggestion that they might come together under one roof. Inexplicably to us at the time, the locally-born young blacks failed to benefit from all this activity. Unwelcome, elsewhere, they flooded into the newly opened Methodist Youth Centre to the near total exclusion of the young whites for whom it had originally been intended. The Methodists, to their infinite credit, accepted the take-over with good grace and a commitment to the fight against prejudice which continues to this day.

Anxious though we all were as to the way things were developing, the issue of race was still seen as part of the overall situation. It was for this reason that Harold Wilson's reply to Powell took the form of an announcement, on 5 May 1968, with a flourish, of the Urban Aid Programme. This was designed to provide funds for inner city regeneration in general and made no mention of the needs of the black community. It was no great innovation except for one thing: Wilson's scheme was based on a 75% contribution by central government provided that the local authority found the remaining 25%. This was the first time central government had ever directly intervened in local authority decision-making. Few of us spotted the significance of this at the time. Indeed, the scheme as a whole made little impact at first. Our hopes of change were fixed on the long-awaited Seebohm Report on the re-organisation of the social services and the current review of the whole system of local government, in both of which I was actively interested. Compared with issues of that magnitude, it seemed a waste of time to argue about the details of Urban Aid.

How wrong we were! Urban Aid proved to be a straw in a wind which was to achieve gale force. Before we grasped what was happening to us, a whirl of activity set in which almost defies description. We had struggled for years to call attention to the desperate plight of the inner areas. At last we had succeeded. 'Save Our City' was the dramatic banner under which the Department of the Environment and the *Sunday Times* organised a prestigious nationwide conference. I was invited, to the chagrin of others who thought themselves better qualified, and added my widow's mite by making sure that no one could ever again plead ignorance of the injustice done to Granby. Inner city regeneration became the 'in' thing. Clearance and new housing estates lost favour as a multitude of proposals for revitalising the inner city took priority. Every public service, every voluntary agency, hurried to lay claim to their right to come to our rescue.

Ironically, one consequence of this official takeover of the burden which we in Granby had previously been left to carry by ourselves was a quite unlooked for enthusiasm for the idea of public participation. For years types like me had nagged on about the importance of involving 'the community' in the management of their common affairs. Bar a few enlightened planners, nobody in particular had listened. Now the tide had turned. Report after report—Skeffington on planning (1968), Seebohm on welfare services (1967), Plowden on pre-school (1967)—had all emphasised the vital importance of public participation in the regeneration of the declining city. The community work that had been going on in Granby became a focus of attention. Officials from both central government and the local authority, representatives of all manner of voluntary agencies and trusts, all clustered round. Political activists came from far and near, as did the media. Community development became a goldmine for academic diggers: Granby was said to be the most researched neighbourhood in the entire UK. Public participation was an essential ingredient in every proposal for action. The phrase featured on every City Council agenda.

Skilled by the experience of the past few years, Granby residents quickly mastered the technique of playing the fruit machine of official aid. I recollect merry gatherings of the Community Council at which, like gamblers in a betting shop, we debated the merits of differing options presented to us. Should we plead our grievous deprivation or our potential as research material or our experience of community work? How best to play off the local authority against the relevant ministry or trust for funding? The Community Council was quick off the mark, and thanks to one of our Labour councillors, the application for Urban Aid for a pre-fabricated community centre in Merlin Street was the first in the city to be approved.

Hopes reached an all-time high with the publication of a report commissioned by Peter Walker as Minister at the newly-created Department of Environment, for a conference in Sweden in 1972. *Fifty Million Volunteers* (London, HMSO, 1972)—the title was both astonishing and self-explanatory. Voluntary service was to lose its do-gooding image. Instead, every single citizen must enjoy as of right the opportunity to become involved in the affairs of their own community.

The enthusiasm for participation spread like wildfire; there were as many as 25 community councils in the city at one point. In the excitement of the moment, few noted the sage comment in the Seebohm Report (op. cit.) that the logical outcome must surely be an increased empowerment of the people. Yet faced with a growing sense of frustration in those of us who struggled to cope with the complexity of the requirements of the separate official departments, this was precisely the question which gradually came to the surface.

Was there really any future in trying to go along with the *status quo* or must there be drastic changes in the system of government as a whole so that it was geared to meeting the needs and wishes of the people rather than those of the party in power? The training courses in community development sponsored by the University's Extra-Mural Department and the LCVS, were eagerly attended by voluntary and statutory workers from all over the city and rapidly developed into a cockpit of debate.

The issue came to a head with the release of a joint report in 1973 by the Community Development Projects (CDP). The CDP teams had been launched by the Home Office in 1968 to explore in a number of inner city areas the practicalities of decentralising the various public services so as to bring them as near to the grass roots consumer as possible. The Liverpool one went to Vauxhall in the north end, Granby being thought to have had more than its fair share of attention. Pooling their experience, the various teams issued a *Joint Interim Report (Forward Plan for 1975–76*, London, CDP Information Unit, Home Office, 1974) in which they argued that the servicing of the inner areas was not a one-off problem but a symptom of a universal malaise which called for a review of the system of government as a whole. This conclusion was received with some reservation locally, less because of a lack of support for the argument than from a nervous suspicion that it stood for Communism. The Home Office, however, were quickly alert to the implications of what was being said. If the conditions in the inner areas were due to the malfunctioning of the machinery of government and not to the inadequacies of those who lived there, then what was required was a major programme of reform, backed by the resources to implement it. Without public discussion, this was assumed to be unrealistic and the CDPs and their report were quietly abandoned.

This effectively marked the turning of the tide of enthusiasm which had powered the community movement in the 1960s. Though throughout the 1970s, ministers of all parties continued to declaim their commitment to the people of the inner areas, as indeed they still do, from then on each service went its own way. Each administration as it came into office tinkered with what had been done before. Each minister announced with pride his own project to end all projects. A tangle of legislation ensued which was all the more difficult to utilise because the rules were so complex and so often contradictory. So far as the bureaucracy was concerned, the problem had been identified and labelled, areas of multi-deprivation had been defined and isolated: all that was required now was that each service should contribute according to its kind, depending on what the Treasury chose to allocate to it. No one seemed to grasp the point my husband had made in his book long years before, that this thrust upon the Treasury a coordinating rôle which it had neither the power nor the wish to undertake. Each department must simply make the best use they could of whatever came their way. The more unsatisfactory the outcome, the more control would fall into the hands of central government. Without more ado, professionals and bureaucrats took over the territory that we had marked out as our own. This was workers' control beyond anything our left-wing colleagues had ever dreamed of.

Gradually, for lack of nourishment, the willingness of local residents to cooperate with officialdom gave place to a tide of protest which increasingly verged on open hostility. Community councils city-wide found themselves elbowed aside by a mushroom growth of pressure groups from which they were excluded by reason of the long-standing embargo on political activity as a condition of grant aid. Increasingly, the centres were absorbed in the struggle for the survival of the bricks and mortar of their premises. Perhaps because it presented a picture of a free-lancing citizenry which cannot have been to the liking of either civil servants or politicians, Peter Walker's remarkable report was discreetly suppressed.

A sense of the irrelevance of 'government' to Granby's affairs crept slowly over people and councillors alike. The local Tory party was dying on its feet as whole streets of its supporters were 'cleared' and rehoused elsewhere. This left the door open for the Liberals whose catch-as-catch-can strategy secured them votes but contributed nothing to the patient reconstruction of the social structure which the community itself had laboured to bring about. My own party gained strength from the amalgamation of Granby with the neighbouring Princes Park Ward, though the zeal of the early days of the Labour Party in that dockside area, which had bred men of the calibre of Eric Heffer, was already faltering.

This was no longer the Granby of the 1960s. The Community Council lamented that it was always the same old handful who carried all the cans but that there were fewer of them now than of old. Such of the stalwarts of SNAP as had not been rehoused retreated into deep dudgeon and disillusion. Churches sadly closed their doors and departed in pursuit of their congregations. Donald May moved on as Methodist ministers must. Phil Doran sought pastures new elsewhere. I myself glumly resigned myself to being the sacrificial victim when the launch of the Merseyside County Council and the redrawing of ward boundaries in 1974 required a reshuffle of our local team.

For me personally, the early 1970s were a time of deepening despondency. Whatever did I think I was achieving by all this ceaseless activity? For years, being a councillor had consumed all my time and thought and energy. Family and friends were swept aside as I rushed hither and thither. The pain of the widening gulf between the ideal to which I still clung and the stark reality of Granby reached an intensity which was almost beyond endurance. As SNAP had so bluntly told me, in words which were to be repeated with uncanny exactitude by the Minister of Merseyside only a few years on, there was no room for the likes of me in the new era of Corporate Man.

Nor for the gallant people in whose service I had apparently laboured in vain. Alienated, pitied, patronised, they were themselves written off as the problem, to whose solution they could obviously have nothing to contribute. I remember accompanying one little group of residents who boldly intruded into a meeting at which the latest new Partnership scheme was to be launched. We are partners—we have come to join in, I politely explained. We were hurriedly bundled out. Partnership was only for officials, we were told. Imperceptibly, the walls of the ghetto were rising all about us. Granby was openly talked of as a troublesome 'colony', ironically enough since the idea of community development had originated in the colonies as a means of containing social unrest.

Reluctantly we found ourselves forced to face the fact that our high hopes that the Welfare State would see the rout of Beveridge's five great giants—want, disease, squalor, ignorance and idleness—were proving to be an illusion. Certainly the Welfare State had put a plank beneath the feet of individuals at risk. But what confronted us now was a giant whose potential for the destruction of our very way of life Beveridge had long ago foreseen. Far from strengthening the bonds of family and community, he had warned, the provision of benefits would simply emphasise the isolation of the individual unless it was off-set by a revitalised sense of obligation to the community as a whole.

> Emphasis on duty rather than assertion of rights presents itself today as the condition on which alone humanity can resume the progress in civilisation which has been interrupted by two world wars and remains halted by their consequences. (William Beveridge, *Voluntary Action*, London, Allen & Unwin, 1948, p. 14)

The opportunity for the exercise of social responsibility must be a right of citizenship, universally enjoyed; this had been our dream and our ambition. This was the distinguishing mark of a free society. Not only had we failed to achieve it but we had lost the very vision which had inspired it. We had been deprived of that most fundamental of the rights of a democratic people, the right to love our neighbours. Years ago, talking of the deprivation of the right of parents to care for their children, Eleanor Rathbone had invented the phrase, 'the disinherited family'. Granby was a disinherited society.

And all the time, remorselessly, deprivation bred deprivation, stress bred stress. As each reacted on the other, the downward slide into desolation went faster and faster. Granby was by now notorious as a society of the unwanted, the left-behind, a population of rejects, the dustbin for the cast-offs of society that one planner assured me was a necessity in every big city. It was a society in a state of chronic flux yet at the same time, one that increasingly found itself trapped in the shrinking area of the Granby Triangle. Chief amongst them were those who found no welcome elsewhere because of the colour of their skin. Imperceptibly the walls of the ghetto were rising all about them. Claustrophobia engulfed us all.

Chapter 10
DEMOCRACY REDISCOVERED

In which I reflect on my experience as Chairman of the Merseyside Police Authority, following the 1981 disturbances. Responsibility for what was done in our name by the police emphasised the importance of accountability. I revert to voluntary action only to discover that there too government by consent has been dangerously eroded. I rediscover democracy at the grass roots.

The move to the new Merseyside County Council in 1974, following the reorganisation of local government, made little visible difference to me. It was a huge relief to be rid of direct responsibility for housing cases, although I still did my share of the 'surgeries'. The pace was leisurely, the style curiously old-fashioned after the rough and tumble of Liverpool City Council. My new colleagues came from all over Merseyside, some with no previous experience of local government, and only a few displayed anything like the aggression characteristic of Liverpool politics. We maintained considerable pomp and ceremony. There were potted plants on the dais of the Town Hall where we held our Council meetings. Our offices occupied the top floors of a tower block down by the Pier Head, with views of such glory that I had to choose a seat with my back to the window to avoid distraction. True, the river was a shining sheet of water empty of all traffic and the cranes of the shipyards pointed skywards in their parking places, but structure planning would remedy all that.

Structure planning! How hard we toiled to plod through the masses of paper and plans placed before us. How diligently the officers struggled to make it all comprehensible to us lay members, with brightly coloured diagrams, presentations and visual aids galore. It was all absorbingly interesting and what a relief to think big after the inward-looking quarrelling of the City Council. All the more so, because it was really nothing to do with us—entertainment disguised as responsibility. For it was the officers who mattered, who knew and understood what was going on. And they in their turn acknowledged their subservience to the 'cabinet' of Chief Officers, an exclusive handful of key figures who, we understood, met in private every Monday morning, presumably to review the decisions to be taken in the week ahead. Nominally at least, they shared their power with our own leaders, a handful of the top men in the party who had seized the key positions though 'seized' is too crude a word for the manipulation by secret caucus which led to their election by the group.

For our first term in office after Labour gained control in 1974, we floundered, trying to discover the boundaries of our new empire as that novel species, a Metropolitan County Council. We had a rag-bag of responsibilities, chiefly to do with the economy of the area as a whole, but including arts and museums where the dream of a rehabilitated Albert Dock kept us happily occupied for years. Most of us were at the end of our political careers. We had no burning vision of the potential of regional government and no wish to do other than live out our last years in peace. An amiable if mildly boring Sunset Village atmosphere prevailed in which like old horses put out to grass, we passed the time very pleasantly. As for those who had elected us to represent their interests, they had no interest in the County and largely ignored our existence. My own Ward had no slot on their monthly agenda for me to report on what I was doing on their behalf.

How remote the County from the here-and-now of the stress of life in Granby. I used to stand at the windows of our mini-skyscraper and there spread out before us like a model in one of our planning sessions, was the literal evidence of the gulf between Them and Us. At the core, tight-packed and exclusive, all the panoply of executive control, the banks, the insurance offices, the paraphernalia of commerce and industry. And as distinct as if an actual city wall still existed, the boundary between what the Bishop, David Sheppard, called the vineyard and the desert without, to which the workers nightly returned in an ugly parallel to the compulsory evacuation of the blacks to the townships of South Africa.

There was, however, one point of common concern between the County and the Ward and that was the worsening relationship between the police and the young, especially the young and black. With the abolition of the old Watch Committee, policing had become a County responsibility though only those of us who represented inner city wards had any grasp of what that might involve. Anger against the excessive use by the police of their power to stop and search on suspicion, had become a commonplace of life in Granby and I was finding it increasingly difficult to accept the evidence of the police in the endless cases brought before those of us who were magistrates. Nor could I go along with the explanation that misdemeanours could be attributed to 'bad apples' in a force that was otherwise all that could be desired.

There was, for instance, the classic case of Lenny Cruickshank who was 'stopped' on the way home from a late-night folk-song session. Questioned as to the ownership of the guitar he was carrying, he ended up in the bridewell charged with the possession of a twist of cannabis which he alleged had been 'planted' on him. The case turned on Lenny's claim that eight officers had been present in the bridewell, one wearing a canary yellow jersey and the counter claim by the police that only six had attended. Melodrama broke out when Lenny spied the missing two officers attending another case in an adjacent court, one wearing a yellow jersey. The case was promptly concluded in Lenny's favour. But for me the consequences were disastrous. I walked home along Lime Street feeling as if the foundations of my life had rocked beneath my feet. That the police, whom I had been reared to regard as my best friends, could lie . . .

My relations with the force were not improved by an investigative programme on Radio Merseyside in the course of which a woman constable bravely told of hearing her colleagues talk of 'going farming' and 'agriculture' as terms for sweeps against the blacks in Granby. Her anonymity proved to be no protection, alas. The police were more interested in silencing her than in dealing with those who had caused offence. I was interviewed by the head of the CID with a view to charging me with suborning her loyalty.

Rather to my dismay, therefore, I found myself chosen by our leader—there was no nonsense about being elected by the group in those distant days—to serve as Deputy Chairman of the Police Authority. Like many of my colleagues, our Chairman found it hard to credit the tales of bullying policemen with their inference that the dream of the British Bobby could possibly be a delusion. He advised against unseemly wrangling and I meekly accepted his ruling, content to plod on at mediation on the basis of the mutual goodwill I assumed to exist. To rubber stamp items put before us at committee, to pay official visits to decrepit police stations of which we had a plethora, to attend the Annual Horse Show in our best garden party finery, this was all that was expected of a good Authority member.

Ironically enough, it was not till 1979, by which time the Tories were in control, that trouble surfaced. Significantly, the bone of contention was not racism but the relationship between the Chief Constable and the Authority. Loyal as they were to their belief that the purpose of having a Police Authority was to support the force—their Chairman actually said as much in public—what stuck in their throats was the arrogance of the Chief Constable. In their book, all chief officers, even the police, must at all times behave with decorum towards elected members. This first came to a head over the death of Jimmy Kelly in the Kirkby police station. The deaths of Blair Peach in Brixton and Liddell Towers in Newcastle had already given rise to a growing apprehension as to the treatment of people held in police cells, so Jimmy's death inevitably attracted attention. Kelly had been on his way home after celebrating his brother's return from Australia. The police having been called, he was taken to the police station where later that night he died. Considerable uproar ensued in the course of which I took the opportunity of a meeting of the Authority to ask the Chief Constable if he would tell us whether the inquiry he had instituted would deal only with the Kelly case or would include all the seventeen other complaints outstanding in Kirkby. No, he declared, he would not and if we wanted further information we could look for it in the local evening paper. It was a bluntness he surely regretted because he subsequently accepted without opposition the proposal I put forward for the setting up of a small sub-committee to monitor the handling of complaints, which, incidentally, proved to be a highly effective cog in the machinery of police accountability.

This naked assertion of autonomy by the Chief Constable was even more forcibly demonstrated when, in response to national financial stringencies, the police budget was cut for the first time ever. What followed was indeed a famous row, conducted in the full glare of media publicity at the behest of the Chief. The Tory Chairman of the County Council actually registered his displeasure publicly in a letter to *The Times* in May 1980. Though the quarrel was discreetly covered up, the dilemma of the relationship between the professional Chief Constable and the lay elected members, which underlay it, was not resolved. Like a peat fire, it smouldered on, an ever-present potential for trouble.

Curiously enough, it was not till Alison Halford, our Assistant Chief Constable, challenged the hierarchy with discrimination some years later, that I realised what my active intervention must have meant for the police (see Alison Halford, *No Way Up the Greasy Pole*, London, Constable, 1993). Bad enough that I was so far past their retiring age—I was in my mid-seventies. Worse that I represented what they regarded as a criminal community. But on top of all that, to be a woman ...! For myself, I was accustomed to assume that women were equal with men, only more so, in the bonny Scots tradition. All my life I had lived in an academic community where women were accepted as colleagues, if not equals. As for the Labour Party, Liverpool was too accustomed to matriarchal governance to bother. Had I at the time but sensed the hostility of the police to having women as colleagues, it might have alerted me to the hidden dangers in my path.

It was against this background of suppressed hostility that Labour won the elections of 1981 and I found myself in the Chair of the Police Authority, our spokesman when in opposition having failed to be re-elected. But for the disturbances only a month or so later, things might have gone on as before. The police would have carried on with their artificial servility, saluting me as 'Marm' and ferrying me around like a ship's figurehead in their large black cars. The elected members would have gone on muttering about the arrogance of the Chief Constable. The alienation of Granby would have continued to gnaw at my conscience. It was only the clamour of those long nights of wild disorder in July that startled us out of our soporific existence.

Our immediate reaction was one of utter incredulity. Even those of us who had forecast violence were stunned by the ferocity of what had happened. A young black community worker came to me in the middle of the night to warn me despairingly that the situation was clean out of control. Whatever should—could—a mere chairman of a committee do in such a moment of crisis? The control of disorder was surely 'operational' and therefore must be left to the police? Thereafter, County officials were far too busy clearing up the debris and organising the public services to bother with elected members. Nobody spared a thought for the Police Authority. My existence was ignored by police and media alike. When Whitelaw, then Home Secretary, came to see for himself, it was only by gate-crashing the lunch at Police Headquarters that I managed to get a word in private with him. Later, when Mrs Thatcher, then Prime Minister, belatedly paid the city a brief visit, I was once more not invited to join the official party to meet her in the Town Hall. Again I gate-crashed and it was on this occasion, after listening to a harangue by her as to how everything must be left to the police that I asked what then was the rôle of the Police Authority? Blank silence followed. I have heard it said that it was at that moment that she determined to get rid of all the Metropolitan Police Authorities.

What abruptly ended this uneasy stalemate was my own spontaneous cry of outrage when, three weeks later, Radio Merseyside rang me early one morning to tell me that a young man had been killed the night before by a police vehicle in the course of further disorder. Only the previous day I had glumly toured the streets of Granby. For all the promises of the VIPs who had descended on us, nothing had changed ... nothing, nothing, nothing had been done ... not even the bins had been emptied. Asked for comment, I cried out in an extremity of despair that they would be fools, apathetic, if they didn't riot.

Even as I spoke, suddenly I understood. What Granby suffered from, what they protested about, was not just poverty or unemployment or bad housing. It was certainly not just the police. Their uprising was a cry of rage against plain, unadulterated, inexcusable injustice. We who governed, elected members, professionals, administrators, had taken it on ourselves to control the destinies of others, not by their consent but by the exercise of power over the machinery of government. They had trusted us and we had betrayed their trust. We had deprived them of their right to responsibility for their own lives and that of the community in which they lived. Against that demeaning of their human dignity, they had a just right to protest. And if we refused to remedy their plight, what alternative had they but to resort to violence, however profoundly deplorable that might be. It was democracy that had failed the people of Granby, not the police.

Here was the answer to the question I had put to Mrs Thatcher. It was the rôle of the police to enforce the law. It was the responsibility of the Police Authority to ensure that justice was done and this we had failed to do.

My comments made the headlines all right. Suddenly all the world became aware of the existence of the Police Authority and of its Chairman. A deluge of publicity descended on me. The media arrived on my doorstep in droves, dangling with equipment, from London, Australia, Norway, Germany. I was quoted and misquoted to distraction. Brian Walden set me up on his *World at One* TV programme as an Aunt Sally for the benefit of the police. Cargoes of hate mail arrived, mercifully balanced by assurances of support from all over the country. The Prime Minister spoke sharply in a House of Commons debate on the irresponsibility of certain persons in positions of authority. Michael Foot gallantly spoke in my defence. Indeed the Labour Party as a whole gave me wonderful support even though not all of them agreed with me. And two local clergy arrived, unsolicited, to answer the 'phone, defend me against intrusion, and do my washing up.

I have told the story of my subsequent experience as Chairman of the Merseyside Police Authority in *Democracy Rediscovered* (London, Pluto, 1988), written while the clang of battle still echoed in my ears. Seen from a decade later, it is clear to me that the need of the media and of the public for a scapegoat—or a champion—swept me off my feet and hurtled me towards a destiny which I never chose and certainly never sought. Willy-nilly, I found myself thrust into the rôle of defender of the right to justice of the individual, a born-again democrat and as such, alternately the object of approbation or deep disapproval. Goliath to my David was the Chief Constable. In all the glory of his well-cut uniform with its shining silver braid, he stood for the supremacy of the law, for stability in an uncertain world, the strong father-figure on whom we could rely in times of anxiety, the protector of society against fear.

So there were the pair of us, personalised by the media like medieval knights, me on my white horse, crying 'Justice' as I galloped into the fray, and he on his black charger—or could it have been a Jaguar?—the defender of the Law. Jointly we symbolised the fundamental dilemma of democratic government in our time; how to respect the autonomy of the professionals and the bureaucrats to whom we necessarily delegate authority without depriving ourselves of our fundamental right to ultimate responsibility for the management of our common affairs.

In the face of unremitting opposition from the force, we settled to the task of coming to terms with our predicament. Experience smartly forced us to concede that it was not for us to run the force ourselves; our job was to see that it was run. This was a staggeringly novel thought to councillors accustomed to take literally the claim that 'we are in control now' after winning an election. In other words, the rôle of the Police Authority was to lay down policy and then to call the police to account for the extent to which they had succeeded or failed in implementing it. Accountability was the instrument of control. And with the shouts of Toxteth still ringing in our ears, it must be accountability to the people and to us as their representatives, and not to the law, the parrot cry of the police.

Easier said than done. The practicalities of implementing this unfamiliar line of thought absorbed most of our time and energy throughout our five years in office. We quickly discovered that the customary annual presentation of a financial budget was useless for our purpose: much more immediate means of monitoring what was going on were required. By trial and error, we built up an eight-point programme, with more in the pipe-line, of ways of making accountability a reality; public forums, lay visits to police cells, an improved complaints' system and so on. Most importantly, the public must have easy access to information on every possible aspect of policing; there must be an end to poker-faced defensiveness. The users must be in a position to speak with an informed voice as to what kind of service they wished to have provided.

At the end of the day, I was satisfied that we had at least laid down the guidelines as to how the principle of accountability by those who provided a public service to the community, whose needs they existed to serve, could be put into practice. At least, the jousting matches between me and the Chief Constable had popularised the idea of accountability so that the word achieved common currency. What's more, we had demonstrated that accountability could work—given the will to make it do so. There was the rub. The police found it wholly impossible to accept the basic principle that they as professionals must be literally accountable to lay people. As they shrewdly realised, if accountability was to be anything more than a courtesy on their part, the elected representatives of the people must be in a position not only to approve or disapprove of the 'accounts' but also to take appropriate action. In other words, if ultimate responsibility rested with the people, and with us as councillors, so must ultimate control.

The police took off in a panic at the very idea. No way could they bring themselves even to discuss the possibility that the resolution to the apparent deadlock might lie in a totally new relationship based on equal partnership. In their book, there had to be a top dog and it was inconceivable that that high office should be occupied by anyone other than themselves. We for our part were equally horrified by the fact that as things stood, the force was, politically speaking, right out of control.

The argument opened up a further dangerous and disturbing issue which we would have had to confront if we had continued in office. If we insisted that the Chief must be accountable to us, what in turn of our own account-ability to those we represented, or, for that matter, to those we employed? It was evidence of their lack of political know-how that the police made little use of this as ammunition with which to counter-attack us. I became acutely conscious of the fact that while the 'ladder' of professional accountability was strong to the point of rigidity, what should have been the complemen-tary line of political accountability was in sad disrepair. It was evident to me that our claim that ultimate control must rest with us as elected representa-tives must surely be matched by our acceptance of the obligation to behave with the utmost responsibility. In fairness, the monitoring of the perfor-mance of the force which we instituted must be balanced by an equally critical monitoring of what we ourselves achieved. The demarcation dispute as to who was accountable for what was an on-going difficulty that could only be tolerable if it was based on the mutual respect and cooperation of equals-in-partnership.

The issue was brought sharply to the fore by the emergence locally of a 'militant' school of thought that was in flat contradiction of all that I was struggling to implement. At first, their passionate assertion that power must lie with the people was refreshing. Gradually however, it became apparent that this stemmed from a cast-iron dogmatism that bore no relation to tradi-tional socialism. Old stagers like myself were startled to find that the people to whom it was proposed to extend power were not the public but only those whom they had elected to represent them. Power must go to the powerful. Victory in the elections was interpreted as a mandate to do whatever the winners thought fit without further reference to those they represented. Once elected, there was no necessity for further consultation with a public whom they seemed to hold in considerable contempt. I could see little difference between them, Mrs Thatcher and the Chief Constable in this regard. Government by elected dictatorship for which they all three stood—to use the classic phrase—was a blatant contradiction of the principle of the universal right to social responsibility to which my whole life had been committed.

The battle was never joined because the return of the Thatcher Government in 1983 effectively signalled the inevitability of our demise, and with it, the end of an era. The hand-over of policing in 1986 to an enfeebled 'Joint Board' was a calculated attack on the very heart of local responsibility. Moreover, the abolition of the six metropolitan county councils meant that the people who lived in those areas were effectively disenfranchised so far as policing was concerned. Few protested. The right to vote for which the women's movement had striven so hard, was as devalued as the old paper pound. All passion seemed to be spent so far as the right to responsibility of the citizen was concerned.

To the people of Granby, the significance of Mrs Thatcher's re-election in 1983 was all too clear as the intangible but unmistakable change in the climate of the streets was quick to reflect. Democracy as they had known it had failed them once too often. There could be nothing in it for them under Thatcherism. The party—or the funeral—was over. Hope fled that day. For years they had consistently recorded their opposition to the irrelevance that was government. They had supported Derek Hatton though they knew that he must fail, for no other reason than that he dared to speak up on their behalf. Now, despairing of government and all its ways, the silent majority simply opted out, retreating into what was a strategy of passive non-cooperation, though it was never put in so many words. The Community Council wilted away in that climate of alienation. The community centre in Merlin Street literally collapsed into its unsound foundations. It was left to the churches to comfort those who found themselves jostled and cast aside.

It was the young and black who stepped into the vacuum thus created. They had taken the lead in opposing the exercise of power by the Militants, alone on Merseyside and at considerable cost to themselves. Now, matured by experience, they announced what was to all intents and purposes, a unilateral Declaration of Independence. A truce to the conventions of traditional politics. They flatly rejected the relegation of Granby to the status of first amongst

Mrs Thatcher's new urban colonies. Go home all ex-patriate whites, government agents and do-gooders. They would do it themselves from now on.

There was no place for me in this new Granby. I was accorded a kindly, even affectionate, welcome at any meetings I cared to attend, but there was no need for an ex-patriate old white woman in that increasingly young black scene. To tell the truth, I was not sorry. Once I had escaped from the treadmill of the chairmanship of the Police Authority, I realised that I had in fact become a full-time unpaid member of the administration. It had offered me scope as an active widow, and I had enjoyed the experience of working with an outstanding team of administrators in the County Council but the exercise of power of that kind was a far cry from the democracy I sought. With the dismantling of local government looming large, councillors were no longer the representatives of the people but were rapidly becoming agents of central government, cogs in a machine over which they had little control. That battle would have to be fought elsewhere. Nor was I prepared to maintain my argument with the police in view of the fact that my loyal deputy had bravely taken on the chairmanship of the emasculated Joint Board which had replaced the Police Authority. I must shift my pursuit of democracy to different ground.

As one door closed, another opened. My absorption in policing and the chronic necessity to defend my back against militancy, had blinded me to what was going on in the world at large. It was to this world that I now returned to a gratifyingly warm welcome; there seemed to be an endless demand for the services of a redundant politician in the field of voluntary work. In the event, membership of various committees quickly turned out to be much more than a way of filling in my spare time as an elderly widow.

I was surprised, though I shouldn't have been, to encounter all over again the identical issues which had for so long absorbed me in policing; the apparently impregnable front of the executive, the gap between government and governed, the fundamental dilemma of how to delegate authority and yet retain responsibility. All that was familiar territory. But this time round, what struck me with savage force was the remarkable change that had come over the voluntary movement as I had once known it. Gone the days when a voluntary worker was a superior person, morally and socially, and paid staff knew their proper place. Gone the reverence for 'the Committee' as representatives of the subscribers, often the sole source of funding. Gone the confident distinction between charity and politics. Most disturbing of all, gone the sense of outrage against the existence of a poverty that was an offence against human dignity and of compulsion on the individual to do something about it.

In their place came a dependence on central government for funding and on professional staff for leadership that smacked of acquiescence, though I was sometimes tempted to use the word subservience. Government was by remote control, not consent. 'They' provided the money and the expertise: 'They' decided what service was needed: 'They' were therefore surely entitled to call voluntary committees to account for what they did with the money that had been given. It was as if the magnetic pole had shifted, throwing all our compasses out of gear. True, there were mutterings of doubt and concern. Conference after conference, which I now had time to attend, was dominated by the apprehension that the voluntary worker was an endangered species, an anachronism in a new age. 'Who is in control?' was a recurrent theme. 'Can we say no?, and, dismally, 'is there any longer a rôle for the voluntary worker?'

However could this have come about? Experience quickly provided the answer. I had kept up a number of my earlier Granby interests and it was through membership of local committees that I began to arrive at an understanding of the here and now with which I found myself confronted. In particular, my association with the voluntary housing movement opened my eyes to what was happening, perhaps because the process of change was more evident in their case than elsewhere. Housing associations had originated with Octavia Hill as a means of demonstrating the potential of efficient and caring management of housing for those in social need (see E. M. Bell, *Octavia Hill*, London, Constable, 1942). They were essentially voluntary bodies, dependent on charitable funding. An opportunity for growth came when in 1969 government grants became available following on the change in housing policy from clearance to rehabilitation to which SNAP had owed its existence. Housing associations acquired a considerable reputation in pioneering this new approach and accordingly, the Housing Act of 1988 heaped on them responsibilities such as the original charities had never dreamed of.

Not only did the volume of work increase, bringing with it a demand for considerably more staff, but the complexity of the grant aid system called for an expertise quite outside the capacity, or indeed the interest, of many voluntary workers. When I was invited to join a local association, I was taken aback by the extent to which the movement had become, in effect, agents of the government. No sooner had I got my feet under the table than I found myself struggling to work out my rôle and responsibilities as a committee member. Shades of the Police Authority! Though there was never a whiff of the arrogance with which the police had treated elected members, there could

be no escaping the exactness of the parallel. This was a world of professionalism, a business and not a charity. Wherever did a voluntary lay committee
come in, other than to rubber stamp whatever was put before us by the emi-
nently trust-worthy staff to whom we had delegated authority to act in our
name?

I soon realised that the voluntary housing movement was no exception to
what had become the rule. My other interests were a mixed bag—race relations, school governance, training for the unemployed, and, of course, youth
and community work—but the lessons to be learned from each were the
same. Put at its simplest, the crux of the matter lay in the relationship between
Them and Us. As a society we had devised machinery for the management of
our common affairs, but somehow, those whom we authorised to run the
machinery had become our masters and not our servants. There was no
room in the system for Us, the people, to assume responsibility. How right
we had been in my student days when in smoke-filled basements we had debated with such earnestness the relationship between the state and the individual. Them and Us; that had been the nub of the matter then; that was the nub
of the matter now. Set in the context of the dissolution of local government
and the abolition of the Police Authority, it seemed to me that what we were
up against was no less than the demise of democracy.

I had assumed that the end of my days as a Councillor would imply my
departure from active politics. With something like incredulity I now realised
that in fact I was right back in the front line where a desperate battle for the
survival of democratic government was in process. The unfinished business
that the Police Authority had not had time to tackle confronted me with
renewed force. Had I the courage, or the conviction, to face up to it? Was I
simply harking back to the dear dead days of long ago? Disheartened, I
contemplated retirement.

Then came Runcorn. The Runcorn Development Corporation had been
set up in 1964 as a government agency to develop a new town on the basis
of the old Runcorn. By 1989 its term of office was reaching its end and the
future administration of the town had to be determined. After much parley-
ing with the government, the four big housing associations on Merseyside
formed the Runcorn Housing Action Group (RUNHAG) whose joint bid
for the entire housing stock was duly successful. Overnight, though that implies a speediness which was deplorably absent from the negotiations, the
association to which I belong found itself landlord to some three thousand
tenants in addition to the four thousand already on their books.

I wish I could claim that the subsequent development that has taken place in

Runcorn, and later in Liverpool, was due to an inspired decision on the part of the committee, but perhaps the truth is even more heartening. For, regardless of who should take credit for what, the outcome is a quite remarkable demonstration of the apparently unquenchable appetite for responsibility of those who would be the first to describe themselves as 'ordinary' people. Given the inch of the government's requirement that residents should be consulted as to who should be their future landlords, the tenants have rapidly acquired a taste for the full ell of total control. As much of the decision-making as is practicable has been delegated to the District Committee, itself a sub-committee of the association's central committee. Well aware of their own inexperience, training in committee work and all aspects of management are provided by professional staff at the request of tenants. As in the case of SNAP, the combination of the sound sense and first-hand experience of the members with the highly professional servicing and commitment by the staff is the secret of the progress that has been made. It has called for a major re-think of their rôles and responsibilities by tenants, staff and the association itself.

Ironically, by destroying local government, the Tory Government would seem to have set in motion a search for a new and different practice of government. The tenants' movement, of which Runcorn is only a single example, is evidence of a rising demand for emancipation from dependence on others for the provision of the basic human needs. It suggests that the future lies in a return to the people of that responsibility for the management of their common affairs of which they are at present deprived. For me, this is the Granby story and the West Indian experience all over again. It is to the grass-roots that we must look for the new growth that will herald a better future. Without roots, no amount of nurturing will produce results.

Part Two

TRACT FOR THE TIMES

In which I argue that the experience of the past century confirms the validity of the principle of the right to social responsibility as a fundamental attribute of universal citizenship. The time has come for a New Emancipation Movement committed to the creation of a Welfare Society of which the Welfare State will be the instrument whereby this privilege will become the daily experience of every citizen.

My tale necessarily comes to an arbitrary halt as narrative of the past gives way to speculation about the future. The forward thrust of developing events will undoubtedly continue but for me, this is a moment for reflection. In the Introduction I lamented the fact that 'we never learn' from past experience. It is incumbent on me, therefore, at this point to demonstrate the relevance of my backward look to the process of planning for the future. What lessons are to be learned from the past, what guidance derived as we make our way into the unpredictable territory of the next century?

I could respond by meticulously itemising every incident in the narrative on which my argument is based because every conclusion I have come to is solidly grounded in my own experience. But to do so would be tedious in the extreme; all the more so because much of my evidence is anecdotal or comes from reports and committee records that are no longer readily available. Instead I propose to leave it to the reader to trace precise relevances while I myself go boldly for the general conclusions to be drawn. What does it all add up to? What is the overall significance of the story I have told? What hope does it offer us of escape from our present slough of despond?

I

When I started out on this book, I expected it to be no more than a worm's eye view of the Welfare State, me being the worm (*A Worm's Eye View of the Welfare State*, Liverpool, Liverpool Council for Voluntary Service, 1993)! It was to be a sequel to my earlier study of the long tradition of charitable effort in nineteenth century Liverpool and the search for an acceptable answer to the problem of continuing poverty in terms of individual charity (*Charity Rediscovered*, op. cit.). I assumed that the outcome would be more or less interesting anecdotage about what it felt like to live through what was effectively a social revolution in the way 'the poor' were dealt with.

To my surprise, as I struggled to reduce the accumulated memorabilia of a long life to something like coherence, it has become apparent to me that a quite different theme has emerged. Instead of being about charity in the traditional sense, my narrative has turned out to be a record of the refusal of all sorts of people in all sorts of circumstances and all manner of places to be deflected from some quite other purpose of their own. Time and time again, I have been struck by an extraordinary sense of some deep undercurrent which obstinately went its own contrary way, dragging me in its wake in flat contradiction of my original intention. I had been, in fact, in danger of imposing my own preconceptions on the activities of the people

I was writing about. I wasn't listening to what they had to say. How often that cry has gone up from the inner cities!

It is only now, when I am in a position to reflect on the whole sweep of the century, that I can begin to comprehend the significance of that undercurrent. It has become apparent to me that neither the relief of poverty nor the attack on its very existence was the real purpose of the people whose endeavours I have tried to record. Indeed, at first sight the theme that has emerged might seem to be only indirectly related to the charitable effort of tradition. What has endowed the whole question of poverty with such priority throughout this century and that which preceded it has not been simply the intolerable burden it imposed on the charity of individuals but the fact that the presence of a continuing and multiplying mass of poverty-stricken people raised in an acute form the much wider issue of the basis on which the affairs of an urban society should be conducted.

This is, in truth, the story of the long slow plod of a community of human beings to adjust to the aftermath of one of the great migrations of our history, that from a rural way of life to an 'urbanicity' never before experienced. The essence of that progress has been the gradual realisation that just as surely as human beings need a roof over their heads and food in their stomachs, so too it is vital that they should enjoy a stable and supportive social framework in which to live out their lives. How singularly appropriate that I should chance to tell my tale in terms of Liverpool, that city of migrants in search of a brave new world!

With astonishment and a growing sense of excitement, I have come to realise that I have not after all been deflected from my original intention but have actually been enabled to set it in a much wider context. For the stuff of that search for a secure framework is the relationship between individuals and the society of which they are members. There can be no charity on a desert island. More than that; it is a hunger for a relationship of a kind that cannot be expressed in terms of state benefits, however generous, or by employment, however lucrative. Material benefits are a means to an end, not an end in themselves. The contract on which that relationship is based, to use the language of today, must comprise giving as well as getting; the obligations and privileges it incorporates must be on a two-way basis. Membership of a society must be such as to enlarge the freedom of the individual and so, in reverse, to enrich the quality of life of all. Or to put it in biblical terms, the relationship between the individual and society is essentially a matter that concerns the need to love your neighbour and to be loved. And what is that but charity rediscovered?

This is not the place, nor am I competent to thrash out the argument as to whether this 'need to belong' is instinctive or has to be acquired. Am I simply rehashing the Presbyterianism in which I was reared? Is it something that is vulnerable to corrosion by economic circumstance or is it much more fundamental than that? I flinch from these challenges and can only reiterate my belief that it is a profound and extremely powerful influence on human behaviour. It is the glue that binds society together.

So to say is not for one moment to deny the existence of the recurrent dilemma of every human society, that of the apparently irreconcilable contradiction between the right to individual freedom and the necessity to accept that, paradoxically, it is a goal which can only be achieved in the context of membership of a human community. The more attention has focused on the importance of personal fulfilment—of which the possessive individualism of today is a blatant symptom—the less thought has been given to the rights and responsibilities of the individual as citizen.

The situation we now face is that we have allowed the gap between the two claims to yawn so wide as to become unendurable. We yearn to be members of a responsible society but the reality is that we have created a system based on stark staring individualism. The consequent sense of helpless frustration and the lack of achievable purpose takes the heart out of living. As every new housing estate demonstrates and events in Toxteth and elsewhere have vividly driven home, given such circumstances, the community disintegrates and protest erupts in the shape of violent disorder and aggression. Clearly what is called for is recognition of the fact that peace of mind lies in striking a balance between the two: as every cyclist knows, progress depends on an equal distribution of pedal power. There can be no either/or; the dilemma must be recognised for what it is, an on-going feature of human existence. Whether the challenge which that constitutes becomes an asset or a liability depends on the extent to which it is boldly confronted and treated as a permanent factor in the making of social policy.

All of which endows with coherence that stumbling progression on the part of a human community that I have attempted to describe in this book. Taken singly, the particular experiences that I recount may appear to be paltry enough. Yet they add up to a striking picture of an evolving society, trying this, abandoning that, but all the time doggedly pursuing a common objective, that of creating a social framework within which the individual can find support and security. Seen in this light the record is not one of random trial and error but a consistent, if often faltering, onward movement by a community of people in pursuit of a dream of common betterment.

It makes sense, too, of all my own miscellaneous scurrying to and fro. To contribute to the building of the community in which I have my being has always been my purpose. I am an instinctive 'socialist', a communitarian, not an individualist. Like the women of the emancipation movement that was my starting point, I long to belong, to find myself through the service of others. And always, like so many women today, I am tormented by the push and pull of the conflicting demands of my need to be myself (ah me, all these courses for women on how to assert them-selves!), as against the hunger for the satisfaction of fulfilling my obligations as a member of a community.

In this context, the message of the past shines out with astonishing clarity. The time has come for us to take our place on that journey of discovery that I have described. The principle of the right of the individual to enjoy the full benefits of membership of a caring society has been established. This is our heritage.

If we are to enter into it, we must now claim our right to share in the creation of such a society, a right which we are at present denied. The opportunity that now challenges us is that of taking the next step forward in what has been aptly described by Michael Meacher, as 'the great historical project of human emancipation' (Michael Meacher, *Diffusing Power*, London, Pluto Press, 1992).

Where do we go from here? As so often before in social history, the logic of events dictates what happens next, a process of which the story of Liverpool provides a singularly appropriate illustration. Early in the nineteenth century, the belief that poverty could be alleviated by spiritual uplift led to an appreciation of the need for environmental improvement. That revealed the necessity for the relief of the individual from the worst stresses of the struggle for survival, hence the long endeavour to create the Welfare State. Out of this in turn has come a grasp of the need for changes in the management of the affairs of the community as a whole. This is the point in the continuum that we have now reached. It is no longer the state of individual 'bad apples' that must be the focus of concern but that of the 'socialising' of the barrel itself; morality has a public as well as a private dimension.

Whether 'socialism' be interpreted as a political party label or taken quite literally as meaning the socialising of social policy, the implication is clear. The priority in social policy from now on must be that of stimulating individuals to band together in pursuit of some common purpose for the public good and making it possible for them to do so. The prime object of our social policy must be to widen our charity from compassion for the welfare of the individual to that of a profound concern for the betterment of the community as a whole. The current mad imbalance between the two must be corrected.

Paradoxically, the lesson we still have to learn is that the self-fulfilment so earnestly desired by the women's movement can only be achieved through membership of a community. Pursuit of justice for the individual necessitates the existence of a just society. A policy of community care implies the existence of a caring community. We have built for ourselves the machinery for the administration of a *welfare state*. Our 'mission' for the coming century must be to match it by the creation of a *welfare society* of which the State will be the servant and not the master. Here is the signpost to the future for which we so urgently seek, here the sense of direction for lack of which we perish in the wilderness.

II

The vision of life in a welfare society is an attractive one. It conjures up a picture of a safe and stable setting within which each and every one can pursue their individual destiny, free to go about the business of life to the best of their ability, confident of their right to full and equal membership of the community on which they depend for their being.

But is talk of this kind like that of Merry England, a day-dream once cherished that must now be relinquished? Is there really no alternative but to accept and accept and accept until the capacity for self-assertion dies a natural death and like cows in a sunlit meadow, we chew the cud of dependence on the state?

So far as the techniques of community building are concerned, the answer is straightforward. Professional training and qualifications in community work have already won recognition in this country and the youth and community service is an established branch of local authority responsibility, though currently under threat from the Conservative Government. As I know from my own first-hand acquaintance, any of the deprived urban areas can provide examples of community development in practice, and to the wealth of their experience can be added that of innumerable developing countries. What is critically absent—as I have heard loudly lamented at many a residents' meeting—is the political will to utilise the skills and experience available to us. For lack of that, all that is offered is a shopping list of random improvements that fluctuates according to the shifts of political power.

The cry goes up for a new Beveridge, a new Plan, new legislation. The media switches its spotlight from one to another of the rising stars in the political firmament. The churches are berated for their failure to provide leadership. The government carries the can for all the ills that beset us. We delude ourselves. To attribute our current malaise to the lack of leadership by individuals of exceptional quality is a cover for our own inertia. Leaders are the product of their times. It is only when they tap some deep well of popular sentiment that they become effective.

Beveridge's own experience proves the point. His Plan won acceptance in flat defiance of opposition from Churchill, then Prime Minister. It was not until popular revulsion against the squalor and degeneration of the years of the Great Depression was brought to boiling point by the encounter with the evacuees from the inner cities that there developed a universal demand that Something Must Be Done. Beveridge's Plan matched that need precisely. It tapped a hidden source of public sentiment that was far more generally and more strongly held than anyone had suspected; it not only set people free from the fear of an old age in the work-house or starvation in the gutter (or whatever), but it also stood for an assurance of community support. The individual was not alone on a desert isle. Society did exist. This was the source of the political will that brought the welfare state into being.

Never has that assurance been more urgently needed than it now is. The fear that haunts us today stems from a universal anxiety that the very framework of community life is disintegrating around us; that the social self-discipline on which we rely far more than we do on the police, is breaking down; that we have little confidence in the capacity or the willingness of the society in which we live to share the load of helplessness and loneliness that is our common lot.

Now, as then, there is a growing sense of unease and dissatisfaction with things as they are. Now, as then, there is a developing awareness that change is overdue. The extraordinary upsurge of feeling provoked by the death of the Labour Party leader, John Smith, in 1994 was a singularly revealing demonstration of the existence of a depth of public sentiment in favour of what can best be described as social morality. People may not want 'socialism', as witness the unexpected outcome of the 1992 election, but a social revolution in attitudes is taking place nevertheless. The eager reception to the latest theory of 'communitarianism' as practised in North America bears this out (Amitai Etzioni, *The Spirit of Community*, London, Simon and Schuster, 1994). Here, undoubtedly, is the deep well of feeling on which we must draw if the political will essential for change is to be generated. It is the realisation of the existence of precisely such an unsuspected resource that is the rewarding outcome of the backward glance over the past century which is the content of this book.

Nevertheless, any hope that this revelation—surely not too strong a word?—will result in political action is immediately doused by the cold reality of the system by which we are governed today. It is a bitter irony that the setting up of the machinery of the welfare state should have contributed to the decline and fall of the dream of the welfare society. Our absorption in system building and the take-over of control by the executive has deprived us of our personal right to social responsibility. The framework of 'connection' between Us and Them, between the individual and the society we live in, has rusted away from lack of use. The futility of rational discussion with a quango is a common experience. My argument has come full circle. We are indeed a disinherited society. Nothing can be done.

The flaw in this reasoning is that we are so groomed to dependence that we forget that the agent of social change is spontaneous voluntary action. No government is elected to contravene its own manifesto. Those who exercise authority are unlikely to favour the diminution of their own power. It is to the gut reaction of the individual—call it conscience or what you will—that we must look for the will to change. This is, however, a factor that slots uneasily into the bureaucratic structure of governance today. There is no scope in our political system for the freelancing voluntary activist, hence the plethora of conferences and inquiries into the role and responsibilities of the voluntary sector. (Shades of my student past!) Nor does it feature in the rather high-flown ambitions of the communitarianism movement.

We have a pretty fair idea as to where we stand as subjects (see Tony Wright, *Citizens and Subjects*, London, Routledge, 1994). Massive legislation piles on us detailed requirements that we have no option but to fulfil. The plethora of misnamed citizens' charters spell out our rights according to the law, though they are noticeably reticent about our responsibility for such laws as are made. But what of our rights and duties as citizens? The active citizen, as defined by the Conservative Party appears to be no more than a loyal subject who voluntarily undertakes to contribute to the common good something more than the statutory minimum. The voluntary worker is equally ill-defined. The traditional image is that of someone who gives service without being paid for it, but this is hopelessly at odds with the reality of the professional-led movement of today.

Whatever the definitions, one point emerges beyond all argument. The nub of the matter lies in the relationship between the individual and the community to which he or she belongs. In a democracy it is a relationship grounded on the ultimate right of the individual to freedom to act according to conscience. Voluntary workers, political activists, the charitable, whatever their objective, are by their actions laying claim to that right. By implication, their role is that of the conscientious objector; they move into action because they dissent from something that is being done or not done in their name, or because they cherish some dream of betterment that is in effect a criticism of things as they are. They are instinctive protestants. Their motives are their own, not subject to external pressure or diktat. Their purpose is to promote the common good according to their lights. The outcome is to bring about social change, though many would deny that that is their intention.

In this context, the relevance of the women's movement to the process of social change takes on a vastly greater significance. The hurly burly of the twentieth century has blurred our grasp of the principles for which the early battle for emancipation was fought. It is generally assumed to have been directed to meeting the needs of a particular group at a particular point in time who suffered from an injustice particular to themselves. With hindsight it is evident that it was never the vote as such that moved women to action, but their grasp of the fact that access to the franchise was the key that would open the door to the opportunity to fulfil their responsibilities as members of society. That was the cause to which they dedicated themselves: it was no one-off effort designed to better their own lives but a demand for admission to their common rights as citizens on behalf of all who were unjustly denied them.

But there was more to it than that. Though women would doubtless have flinched from the thought of putting it in so many words, what their demand really amounted to was an extension of political power to a group that had previously been denied it. Subsequent experience has taught us that if responsibility is to be effective in practice, it must necessarily carry with it the power to take remedial action. I have watched with fascination how, within my own lifetime, the plea for social responsibility by middle-class women has crystallised out into an all-inclusive demand for 'power' for the community as a whole. Thus defined, the customary assumption that voluntary service is a privilege of the leisured and the affluent has no relevance to today. The voluntary worker stands revealed as an equal citizen.

This is the point we are now at. The next step must be to articulate the vague demand for empowerment in plain language. There must be an end to the pussy-footing mystique that clouds the discussion of voluntary action. Talk of voluntary work as a fringe benefit of government, a virtue and not a necessity, an optional extra on the part of the active citizen—all that must give way to a bold declaration of intent. In its place there must be open recognition of the fact that an extension of responsibility, which is the purpose of emancipation, implies an extension of political power the practical implications of which must be openly acknowledged. The demand for increased responsibility and the power that necessarily accompanies it must be recognised for what they are, an extension of the rights and duties of citizenship.

III

The time is surely ripe for the launching of a New Emancipation Movement that will liberate us as citizens from the entanglements of a bureaucracy which frustrates our every intention and will set us free to explore with enthusiasm the relevance of our heritage of social responsibility to the challenge of the coming century. There is desperate need for a focus to be provided for all the multifarious endeavours of that great freemasonry of those we call voluntary workers, which will weld them together into a coherent and powerful force. That focus can only be dedication to a common cause. And that cause must be a powerful assertion of belief in the principle of the universal right to social responsibility as an attribute of citizenship.

The immediate task of a new emancipation movement must therefore be to articulate these vague aspirations in terms of a clear objective and a practical strategy for achieving it. Is it fanciful to suggest that 'Votes for Women' as a rallying call might perhaps be replaced by a demand for 'More Power To the People'? As for strategy, the way ahead is clear. Social responsibility and political power are the perquisites of a citizen, not a do-gooder. To enhance the rights and responsibilities of the citizenry is a political objective. Political action will be required to achieve it. Those who seek empowerment must face up to the realities of politics. The so-called voluntary movement must 'go political'.

This is a proposition from which the established voluntary agencies and communitarians alike start back in horror. Their protestations stem from a lamentable incapacity to grasp that to opt out of governance is simply not practicable: even the decision as to whether or not to do so is itself a political gesture. Few of them are willing to admit that by participating in the contract culture they inextricably involve themselves in politics—and party politics at that. Yet the Thatcherism that has corrupted the values that characterise the voluntary movement is an unconcealed expression of a straightforward political dogma; it can only be countered by an equally forthright reaffirmation of the political morality on which voluntary action is based. This is sadly lacking from the present debate about the future—if any—of voluntary work: no wonder the volunteer of tradition is an endangered species. If this wilful refusal to recognise the reality of political life is to be overcome, it is essential that the antipathy to politics and politicians be corrected. This must be a priority for the a new emancipation movement.

Paradoxically, this blanket disillusion with party politics has given rise to a contrary zest for political action of which the classic example is the astonishing outburst against the poll tax which brought out on to the streets people who had never before taken part in any kind of joint action.

If this surge of political activity is not to settle into a dangerous pattern of chronic frustration and eventual open hostility, it is essential that opportunities be provided to enable individuals to make an effective contribution to the governance of the country. The next step must therefore be to organise the management of our common affairs so as to permit of full acceptance of their social responsibilities by every citizen. The ludicrous inequity of the participation that passes for partnership is simply not enough. The 'building of bridges' so much lauded by the police, is no more than a sop to public opinion. Put at its simplest, the voice of social conscience—the voice of the citizenry—must be recognised as a third force in government.

To talk of the citizenry as a third force in government is most emphatically not, let me hasten to interject, a plea for the setting up of some monstrous new ministry or raft of futile quangos, trailing in their wake yet another regiment of bureaucrats. Nor am I suggesting the creation of some assembly of the great and the good who presently constitute the governance of the voluntary agencies. On the contrary, the target must be nothing less than the full-blooded integration of the citizenry into the system of government on an equal but different footing from that of the political parties or the bureaucracy.

How to translate the theory into practise? The answer is surprisingly simple, and, indeed, on the basis of the story I have told, obvious, though the implications are complex and far-reaching. The justification of the demand for more power to the people is that it is a demand for more responsibility. If empowerment is to be anything more than tub-thumping, it must carry with it the power to call to account those to whom authority to act has of necessity been entrusted. Lip service is paid to this as a theory: committees are deluged with what purport to be evaluations of outcomes. What is lacking is acceptance of the corollary; if the account rendered is rejected as not satisfactory, then the delegation of authority to act can be modified or cancelled at the discretion of whoever delegated it in the first place.

It is the near-universal failure to put this principle into practice that is the main cause of the widening gulf between Us and Them, citizen and city, subject and state. Commendable efforts are made to bridge the gap between those who provide services and those called customers, but they are invariably defeated by argument as to where ultimate responsibility rests. (The endless disagreement between the Merseyside Police Authority and its force was at bottom a debate about this very issue). The principle that in a democracy, responsibility finally lies with the people is difficult to deny but hard to put into practice. This was what the women's movement sought to establish. This is what the drive for more power to the citizen is all about. The demand for the empowerment of the citizenry will be futile unless it carries with it effective responsibility for what is done in their name.

To put this principle into practice need not necessarily call for riot or revolution. The machinery for democratic government is already in place, though in constant need of overhaul and servicing. What renders it useless is the way we work it. The fatal flaw is that the key to the switch that activates it has been handed over to those to whom we have delegated responsibility for its operation. Control, and with it responsibility, has passed to that medley of operators we refer to as 'Them'. (I was dumbfounded to discover the extent to which governance of the police is by workers' control.) The demand for the empowerment of the people stands for a reversal of this situation, a simple claim but one which rouses fierce opposition.

The old familiar cry immediately goes up from all those whose grip on the levers of control is would threaten—be they parents, politicians or establishment figures—that 'they aren't ready for it yet': this provides justification for the new colonialism which now dominates social policy towards the inner areas. It is bolstered by the argument that the public fail to respond when given the opportunity to participate. There is no perception of the possibility that this is in fact evidence of the failure of those in authority to appreciate that altruism (which is what citizenship is all about) grows by what it feeds on. Nor that the atrophy bred by long years of alienation from responsibility cannot be overcome by timid invitations to 'consult' about decisions already taken. Only the experience of full and active integration will stimulate an awareness of community responsibility.

Equally crucial to the success of any attempt to increase the power enjoyed by the people—and this is not optional but an absolute essential—is the correction of the ludicrous inequity of the existing relationship between Them and Us, the governors and the governed. How often have I cringed to watch the rout of some sturdy but inadequately resourced group of public-minded persons when confronted by the massed experience and expertise of those in authority. If the citizenry are to make a valid contribution to government, they are in justice entitled to a level of support and servicing equivalent to that of those whose partners they are invited to become. Access to information and impartial advice on how to use it, together with the physical and financial resources necessary for any kind of joint action are prerequisites of an educated democracy. There is substance in the argument that power in the hands of an uneducated people may well be a greater threat to good government than a dictatorship.

All well and good; so much is common currency among those concerned with community development. The need for education is widely supported and a whole new breed of trainers and facilitators has come into being to meet the demand. It is, however, noticeable, that their assumption of authority is seldom questioned; as professional practitioners it is taken for granted that they should hand on what they themselves have profitably practised. Bishop Jenkins has wryly commented on the arrogance with which the *politicos* who manage our affairs treat the *idioticos* whom they exist to serve (David and Rebecca Jenkins, *Free to Believe*, London, BBC Books, 1991).

Yet the truth is that however expert our mentors may be in market-place know-how, their grasp of what makes a human society 'tick' and how the machinery of governance actually works is frequently abysmal. Consequently, empowerment, as it is currently implemented, tends to look remarkably like a contemporary version of the age-old patronage of the poor It is assumed that all those with social needs are powerless because they are poor and that therefore the training they need is that which will enable them to find work. Whereas the truth is that if we are to function as a society and not a random collection of self-seeking individuals, our target must be the political one of the extension to all and sundry of the rights and duties of citizenship. This is what empowerment is all about; it must comprise not only those who are poor but the entire community, governors as well as governed. If we are to enter into the heritage of social responsibility of which we are presently deprived, the standard of our skill in managing our affairs, for which Granby coined the word *politeracy*, must be universally improved.

To put such a programme into practice need not necessarily result in riot or mayhem. Experience suggests that we start from where we are and not from where we would like to be. A wholesale transference of power by melodramatic new legislation and changes to the constitution will achieve little tangible result at grass roots level. Empowerment can best be achieved by evolution, not revolution. Progress will depend on the cultivation of an appetite for responsibility as and when and where the opportunity occurs. The widespread hostility to any talk of political involvement will only be overcome by actual experience of it; action education has long been recognised as the most successful method of stimulating interest. The disruption of local government has deprived us of our customary chance of involvement. An enlightened opportunism must be the order of the day.

Much will depend on the response of all those who are now in a position to exercise control. A major change of heart will be required of them. There must be an end to the insufferable patronage by those in authority (many of whom themselves work in the voluntary sector) whose notion of partnership consists of permitting the presence amongst their numbers of a token beneficiary, preferably a woman, preferably disabled, but essentially black. Like the parents of growing children, those who manage our society must accept that the time has come to hand over the keys of the front door. They must put their professionalism and their experience at the service of those from whom their authority is derived. Above all, they must exhibit an unquenchable respect for the right to responsibility of every single citizen regardless of status or merit. Everything they say or do must bear witness to their regard for the people they exist to serve and to their own commitment to enabling them to live up to their responsibilities.

It is the duty of the state to see to it that this comes about. To draw the line between enabling the free development of voluntary initiative and dictating the direction along which it shall develop will call for a highly principled stand on the part of those in positions of authority. The role of the executive must be recognised for what it is, the instrument for implementing the wishes and meeting the needs of those with whom ultimate responsibility rests, the servant of those from whom their own authority is derived. The community, that nebulous yet real entity, must be enabled and encouraged to formulate a code of values for itself; this is as far as intervention from outside must be allowed to extend. The servant state is not there to do good to its people but to make it possible for them to do good to others. Public services must be just that: services designed to meet public requirements as determined by those who use them. (What a difference this would make to policing policy!) The giving of grant aid must be directed to the promotion of independent action on the part of the citizen and not to that of party dogma. The state must stimulate the provision of opportunities but draw back from using this as patronage or a subtle exercise of control.

IV

So much for what ought to be or could be (for which the demand is perhaps more universal than we realise), yet set against the contemporary political scene, it is hard to resist the temptation to write it all off as pie in the sky. Judging by past experience, all that will come of 'empowering' the people will be yet further proliferation of the bureaucracy such as has obscured the true purpose of the welfare state. In the face of the glum prognostications with which we are deluged, what message of hope, what wisdom for future guidance, can I derive from the opportunity afforded by old age to reflect on the lessons of the long span of my life and times?

For myself, I am content that I have at least acquired a better understanding of both the dilemma and the potential of the search for personal self-fulfilment as against the need to be a contributing member of the society—a conflict that has been both a source of, and a stimulus to endeavour, all my life, all the more so because I am a woman. The quest for understanding has certainly brought me something like peace of mind. The pursuit of wisdom is an infinitely desirable way of life and one to which I could happily have committed myself by retreating into the ivory towers of the nearby university (though in fact it is built of redbrick with majolica tiles). But for one thing, and that one thing is the sum and substance of my entire experience, namely, that the urgency of my 'need to belong' by sharing in the common endeavour to create a better society has been an even more powerful influence than has been my search after personal survival and fulfilment. The dawning recognition of the fact that resolution of that apparently irreconcilable dilemma lies in 'loving my neighbour better than myself' is what has inspired me to commit myself to the fight for social change.

It is the realisation late in life that I am not alone in this quest for peace of mind that gives me hope. I have discovered—and the word is singularly apt to the way I have lived my life—that the constant struggle to balance the two drives is in no way unique to myself but is an on-going and universal experience that underlies every human existence. On the basis of that understanding I have come to believe with all the passion of total conviction that the urge to belong to a secure and supportive social framework and to contribute to its creation constitutes the one force that can overcome the greed and arrogance of a society dedicated to individual self-interest. Faith in the dream of life in a better society alone provides the hope that makes life worth living. Our very survival as a human community depends upon it. Without that vision, the people must surely perish.

There are those who argue that the pendulum has swung so far towards individualism as to be beyond reversal. In reply, I can only reiterate my conviction that the 'need to belong' is so fundamental to human existence that it cannot be destroyed—diminished or distorted perhaps, but never totally extinguished. I believe that the time must come when the urgency of the demand for social change will reach such an intensity as to constitute an irrefutable requirement. It was the desperation of the need for change demonstrated by the disturbances of 1981 that impelled me out of obscurity into a totally unforeseen assumption of authority. I was given no option. The pattern is a repetitive one. The swell of public feeling will itself throw up the necessary leadership.

It is the vindication of that belief by the actions of the people I have been called on to serve as a politician and voluntary worker that has constantly refreshed my loyalty to my heritage and enabled me to survive the hazards of life. And it is on that basis that I find grounds for optimism in the groundswell of do-it-yourself spontaneous action on the part of innumerable ordinary citizens, who refuse to be deprived of their right to find themselves in the service of others. However inarticulately, they demonstrate the constancy of the search after what it means to be a citizen in an urban democracy which has given purpose to the century that is ending and in whose continuation lies our best hope for the future. What they have to offer is no final solution but a way of life. It is the way that will lead us forward into the future.

The road ahead will be rough and dangerous. There will be casualties. Confrontation with what is strange will bring pain to those who remember the past with nostalgia. Nevertheless, I believe that if we are loyal to our heritage—if we claim it with passion and conviction—the upshot will be such as to take us one step further along our way to the achievement of that stirring vision which Beveridge himself set before us in the final sentence of his great trilogy:

> So at last, human society may become a friendly society, each linked to all the rest by common purpose and by bonds to serve that other purpose. So the night's insane dream of power over other men, without limit and without mercy, shall fade. So mankind in brotherhood shall bring back the day. (Beveridge, op. cit.)

BIBLIOGRAPHY

BOOKS AND REPORTS

Bell, E. M., *Octavia Hill*, London, Constable, 1942.

Beveridge, William, *Voluntary Action*, London, Allen & Unwin, 1948.

Beveridge, William, *Power and Influence*, London, Hodder & Stoughton, 1952.

Booth, Charles, *Life and Labour of the People of London*, London, Macmillan, 1883–1903.

Community Development Programme, *Joint Interim Report (Forward Plan for 1975–76*, London, CDP Information Unit, Home Office, 1974.

Department of the Environment, *Fifty Million Volunteers*, London, HMSO, 1972.

Etzioni, A., *The Spirit of Community*, London, Simon and Schuster, 1994.

Girvan, D. T. M., *Working Together*, Kingston, Institute of Jamaica, 1993.

Halford, Alison, *No Way Up the Greasy Pole*, London, Constable, 1993.

Harvey, Audrey, *Tenants in Danger*, Harmondsworth, Penguin, 1964.

Hope, E. W., *Health at the Gateway*, Cambridge, Cambridge University Press, 1931.

Hunt, Lord (Chairman of Committee), Department of Education and Science, *Immigrants and the Youth Service: Report of a Committee of the Youth Service Development Committee*, London, HMSO, 1967.

Ireland, Ivy, *Margaret Beavan of Liverpool*, Liverpool, Henry Young, 1938.

Jenkins, David and Rebecca, *Free to Believe*, London, BBC Books, 1991.

Jones, Caradog., *Social Survey of Merseyside*, Liverpool, Liverpool University Press, 1934.

Jones H. and Muirsheald, J., *Life and Philosophy of Edward Caird*, Glasgow, Maclehose Jackson, 1921.

Keeling, Dorothy, *The Crowded Stairs*, London, National Council of Social Service, 1961.

Kelly, Thomas, *For Advancement of Learning: The University of Liverpool 1881–1981*, Liverpool, Liverpool University Press, 1981.

King, Constance M. and Harold, *The Two Nations: The Life and Work of Liverpool University Settlement and its Associated Institutions 1906–1937*, Liverpool, Liverpool University Press, 1938.

Kitchen, Paddy, *A Most Unsettling Person*, London, Gollancz, 1975

Liverpool City Planning Department, *Social Malaise in Liverpool*, Liverpool, Liverpool City Council, 1967.

Liverpool Youth Organisations Committee, *Special But Not Separate*, Liverpool, 1968.

Macadam, Elizabeth, *The Social Servant in the Making*, London, Allen & Unwin, 1945.

Macadam, Elizabeth, *The New Philanthropy*, London, Allen & Unwin, 1934.

MacCunn, John, *Liverpool Addresses on Ethics of Social Work*, Liverpool, Liverpool University Press, 1911.

Mackay, J. M., *A New University*, Liverpool, Liverpool University Press, 1914.

May D. and Simey, M., *The Servant Church in Granby*, Liverpool, Centre for Urban Studies, University of Liverpool, 1989.

Meacher, Michael, *Diffusing Power*, London, Pluto Press, 1992

Midwinter, Eric., *Priority Education*, Harmondsworth, Penguin, 1972.

Personal Service Society, *Annual Report*, Liverpool, 1922.

Plowden, Lady (Chairman of Committee), Department of Education and Science, *Children and their Primary Schools: A Report of the Central Advisory Council for Education*, London, HMSO, 1967.

Poole, H., *The Liverpool Council of Social Service 1909–1959*, Liverpool, Liverpool Council of Social Service, 1960.

Raleigh, Sir Walter, *A Miscellany*, Liverpool, Liverpool University Press, 1914.

Rathbone, E. F., *William Rathbone*, London, Macmillan, 1905.

Rathbone, Eleanor, *The Disinherited Family*, London, Edward Arnold, 1924.

Rathbone, Eleanor, *The Ethics and Economics of Family Endowment*, Social Service Lecture Trust, Epworth Press, 1927.

Rathbone, William, *Social Duties, By a Man of Business*, London, Macmillan, 1867.

Reilly, C. H., *Scaffolding in the Sky*, London, Routledge, 1938.

Robbins, Lord (Chairman of Committee), *Report of the Committee on Higher Education*, cmnd 2154-1, London, HMSO, 1963.

Seebohm, Frederic (Chairman of Committee), *Report of the Committee on Local Authority and Allied Personal Services*, cmnd 3703, London, HMSO, 1968.

Shelter Neighbourhood Action Project, *Another Chance for Cities—SNAP 69/72*, Liverpool, SNAP, 1972.

Simey, M., *Charitable Effort in Liverpool in the Nineteenth Century*, Liverpool, Liverpool University Press, 1951, reprinted as *Charity Rediscovered*, Liverpool, 1992.

Simey, M., *Democracy Rediscovered*, London, Pluto, 1988.

Simey, M., *A Worm's Eye View of the Welfare State*, Liverpool, Liverpool Council for Voluntary Service, 1993.

Simey, T. S., *Principles of Social Administration*, London, Oxford University Press, 1937.

Simey, T. S., *Welfare and Planning in the West Indies*, London, Oxford University Press, 1946.

Smith, Austin., *Journeying with God*, London, Sheed & Ward, 1990.

Stocks, M. D., *Eleanor Rathbone*, London, Gollancz, 1949.

University of Liverpool, Department of Social Science and Liverpool Council for Voluntary Service, *Our Wartime Guests—Opportunity or Menace?*, Liverpool, 1940.

Victoria Settlement, *Annual Report*, Liverpool, 1903.

Victoria Settlement, *Annual Report*, Liverpool, October 1908.

Webb, Beatrice, *Our Partnership*, Cambridge, Cambridge University Press, 1915.

Wright, Tony, *Citizens and Subjects*, London, Routledge, 1994.

PERIODICALS

Brown, H. P., 'Memoir of A. M. Carr Saunders', *Proceedings of the British Academy*, 1967.

Liverpool Quarterly, 1933.

Mackenzie Dr Leslie, *Liverpool Daily Post*, 18 May 1913.

Manchester Guardian, May 1933.

Phelps, Miss, 'An Enquiry in Connection with Underfed School Children', *Transactions of the Economic and Statistical Society*, Liverpool, 1906.

Rathbone, Eleanor et al., in *Transactions of the Economic and Statistical Society*, Liverpool, 1907.

The Recorder (University of Liverpool), November 1973.

Reynolds, Gillian, *Arts Alive* (Liverpool), June 1972.

'Stones for Bread', *Liverpool Courier*, 15 February 1909.

University College Magazine (Liverpool), Vol. 3, 1887.

INDEX